RARE FLOWER

Dignity Press
World Dignity University Press

Ada Aharoni

RARE FLOWER

Life, Love and Peace Poems

Dignity Press
World Dignity University Press

Parts of this book were published before in Hebrew under the title "Perah Nadir" by Rimonim Publisher, Israel, 2012, and in English, under the title "The Pomegranate", by 1st Books Library, 2002, United States.

Published by Dignity Press
16 Northview Court
Lake Oswego, OR 97035, USA
www.dignitypress.org

Book website: www.dignitypress.org/rare-flower
Book design by Uli Spalthoff
The photo of Talia Aharoni Winkler on the cover was taken by her mother, Ada Aharoni.
Most of the pictures in the book were taken by Haim, Ada, Talia and Ariel Aharoni, or by other members of the family.
Photo of Vincent Van Gogh's Sunflower painting on page 48: Wikimedia (The Yorck Project: 10.000 Masterpieces of Painting)
Flower graphic by Joana Castro Teixeira

Printed on paper from environmentally managed forestry: www.lightningsource.com/chainofcustody

ISBN 978-1-937570-10-1
Also available as EPUB: ISBN 978-1-937570-11-8
and Kindle eBook: ISBN 978-1-937570-14-9

In Memory of Haim and Talia

Happiness is to share life,
thoughts and creations with
loved ones

Contents

Ada Aharoni at the signing of her first book:
"Poems from Israel", in Boston.

PREFACE

The Universal Poet of Love and Peace
Ada Aharoni Shares Her "Rare Flowers"

A moving collection of poems by poet Ada Aharoni expressing new human depths of love and vivid visions of a world beyond war

In a unique collection of poems entitled RARE FLOWER: Life, Love and Peace Poems, poet and author Ada Aharoni, the "Woman of No Time," brings a message of love and peace to a world often at war with itself, to men and to the women who give life to the children. She dedicates her book to the memory of her two departed loved ones: Talia, her daughter who recently died of cancer, and Haim, her husband.

Full of moving and vivid descriptions and clever mastery of lyrical poetic innuendoes, "Rare Flower" follows existential key themes throughout the book. As a woman and mother, Aharoni celebrates love and denounces war in theory and in practice. She condemns the senseless deaths of soldiers and notes the perils of war in an age where nuclear attack is possible and "can dangerously lead to the end of humanity."

Despite her ominous lyrical warning, her book is full of hope. It focuses on the possibility of peace between cultures and creeds: Jewish, Muslims and Christians, Israelis and Palestinians, and the creation of "A Global Village Beyond War."

Ada also shares with us her exciting and moving travels around the world, through her humanistic, innovating and significant lens.

Called the "poet of love and peace," Aharoni has published 12 poetry books to date, and 16 novels, biographies and books for children. She writes in English, Hebrew and French, and her works have been translated into 17 languages. Peace and conflict resolution are recurrent themes throughout all her works. She is a writer, poet and peace culture researcher, who strongly believes that "Culture and literature can help us in healing the urgent ailments of our global village, such as war, conflict, terror, famine and problems of environment." Poetry is one of the best vehicles to do so, as it has the ability to reach the deepest levels of feelings, consciousness and thoughts, in a way that no history books and no politics can achieve. Aharoni tells us that Poetry has the ability to build bridges of understanding and reconciliation between people and nations, and this is what "Rare Flower" brilliantly achieves with each one of its "ruby grains."

Ada Aharoni is both Israeli and French, but she considers herself a Global Citizen. She was born in Egypt, and now lives in Nesher, Israel, and she often flies to Paris to visit her family. She attended Birkbeck College at London University in England and received an M.Phil. Degree in English literature, on the novels of Henry Fielding. She was awarded her Doctorate Degree on the works of Nobel Prize Laureate Saul Bellow, from the Hebrew University in Jerusalem. She has received many prizes and awards, including the British Council Prize for Poetry, the World Poetry Golden Crown Prize, and the President Shimon Peres Award for spreading the Culture and Literature of Peace (Jerusalem, 2012).

She has also been elected one of "*The 100 Global Heroines*" in Rochester, New York, in 1998. She is the founder and world president of "*IFLAC:* The International Forum for the Literature and Culture of Peace", and its women's wing: "The Bridge: Jewish and Arab Women for Peace in the Middle East". She also presides over *Shlomit* – the IFLAC children's branch for peace. Her videos on her work in IFLAC and her research on "*The Second Exodus:* A New Way To Promote Peace Between Israelis And Palestinians", are in *Youtube,* and have been highly praised. There one finds, as well, several of her poems from "Rare Flower" that have been put to music and are sung by composer and singer Shoshia Beeri-Dotan, who has been compared to singer Joan Baez.

Ada Aharoni is also the editor of the online *IFLAC Digest*, and two innovative and important series of peace culture and literature anthologies: *Galim (Waves)*, and the online *Horizon*. Readers are invited to visit her websites: www.iflac.com/ada, www.iflac.word press.com and www.iflac.com/ada/heb. She can be contacted for interviews and feedback at: ada.aharoni06@gmail.com

FOREWORD: MY TWO RARE FLOWERS

Last year I lost my most precious treasure, my daughter Talia, my so unique "Rare Flower". Since, there is a white mist enveloping an infinite horizon of deepest aching and longing in the heart of the garden of my life.

Talia was a very special person, a spring of angelic goodness, intelligent, beautiful and so creative! She had the marvelous ability to create joy, happiness and beauty all around her, to wonder at every petal of every flower and to smilingly offer them to us to keep in our hearts forever.

Together with her so loving and devoted husband Avi, Tali created a family of love. She was sweet, gentle and modest as well as a rock of courage, determination and strength. She confronted all difficulties with her enchanting smile, including her sickness. She took great care of her health, and thoroughly studied her cancer, coaxing it into giving her a prolonging of thirteen full and fruitful years, in which she sang and directed the Nofit Choir, joyfully danced folkloric dances, and lectured on the "Importance of the Development of Memory," at the exemplary Dorot Center which she founded and directed.

Everybody loved and admired Tali. Those thirteen years gave her the time she so needed to help her three children grow tall and strong, as blossoming palm trees full of promising dates, and she was there with them when the boys, Itai and Ori terminated their army service, and went to college, and when her beloved daughter Nitzan finished school and was mobilized in the army. A year before she passed away, Tali also enjoyed the fulfillment of her greatest wish - embracing the birth of her tiny, delightful granddaughter Lotem.

Lately, I received a letter written by somebody I do not know, who read the Hebrew version of the book "Rare Flower" – "Perah Nadir", and who wrote to me:

"Dear Ada, your poems and your tears have brought Talia back to life, and even though I did not have the pleasure of meeting her, she lives in my mind as the gentle and peace loving person who gave so much of herself for others. Talia has made me a better human being. Peace will come soon and the future generations will remember that on this day Talia was reborn and given life through words and "Rare Flower" poems…"

These words filled me with the radiant sunshine of her presence and vital influence even though she is physically not with us anymore. In the following pages you will find poems in memory of Talia, as well as poems which she specially appreciated. Talia is intrinsically part of most of them, as her love of humanity, peace and harmony is at their very basis. Indeed, memory and words can conquer death, and Talia will live not only in our memory, but also in words and poems about her.

The present book is also dedicated to my dear departed husband Haim, Talia's father, whom she loved so much, and who died on 7th July 2006. It is as if Talia hastened to meet her father, when five years later, on the 8th of July 2011, she left us for her mysterious journey, from which she did not come back.

Haim was a very special and loving person, extremely intelligent, with a fully humanistic and scientific soul, who believed that through science we can create a better world. He was an appreciated and greatly admired scientist at the Technion in Haifa: "Israel's Institute of Technology", and he was often invited to share his research and his innovating papers abroad in prestigious universities around the world. He was always rational and kind, and he had a wonderful sense of humor that Talia inherited.

Both Haim and Talia helped me a great deal with the conception and the founding of "IFLAC: The International Forum for the Literature and Culture of Peace." It was founded near the end of the previous mushroom millennium in 1999, as a voluntary association, with the great hope that the opening of the next millennium would see a world beyond war, terror and famine.

Haim and I fully enjoyed our fifty five years of our fruitful life together with the two children Talia and her elder brother Ariel, who is today a doctor of Gynecology at the Rothschild Hospital in Haifa. When Talia was a tot, whenever she saw Haim and me hugging each other, she used to budge in between us and say: "What about me? I want to be hugged and kissed too!" So we joyfully picked her up and showered her with our loving kisses and hugs. But this was not enough for Talia, who with her heart of gold always cared about others: "And what about Ariel", she asked, "He wants to be hugged and kissed too!" So the four of us hugged and kissed and joyfully sang and waltzed the dance of life together in our happy home. Today, there are sadly only two of us left of this joyful quartet.

I dedicate this book to my two departed "Rare Flowers", not only in their memory, but also in their honor, as examples of fine, brilliant, rational and kind human beings who should be imitated. If there were more good, creative and loving people like Talia Aharoni Winkler and Haim Aharoni in our world, our global village would be a safer, better and a much more loving planet.

Ada Aharoni

ada.aharoni06@gmail.com

www.iflac.com/ada
www.iflac.wordpress.com
www.iflac.com/guestbook

Ada and Haim at their wedding

PART ONE

LOVE POEMS

Life Is A Pomegranate

Life is a Pomegranate my friend
A world of Plenty
Full of juicy ruby grains –
If you search for them.

When you find them
Taste them fully
One by one
Long before
They become –
No more.

Ada Aharoni

CAKES AND POEMS

You brought the cake,
and I the poem.
We read the cake,
and ate the poem.

My wishes pass
through pierced ear-lobes,
so much helpless groping
to keep us more together,
to walk beyond the sidewalks,
to make us whole.

I see a postage stamp world
where your postcard
has not arrived;
sometimes a green bile stone,
sometimes a song.

White magnolias break into my night –
above all it is your sound I hear.
I drink the dawn.
Your sound is a calm river
of copious silky kisses.

Laughingly, our glances lock.
It is almost worth parting
to meet again –
I blow the Shofar*.

You will go on bringing the cakes,
and I the poems.

Enjoy life with a woman you love
all the days of your life.
Ecclesiastes 9:9

* Traditional ram's horn

Ada Aharoni

IN THE SUN

She took him
to the sun
with a pigeon
on his shoulder
a smile in his eye
a song in his ear,
clutching his throat
through the woods
of trembling –
where he fell in love
with his sun-laden dream,
a ring of laughter
on his finger,
a fragrant kiss
his moist fresh
life.

THE MARRIAGE OF SCIENCE AND POETRY

Mr. Einstein, notable shadkhan,*
Science to Poetry benevolently presented.
For Science it was love at first sight,
but while he persisted the lady held back and desisted.
"Our impulses are parallel," he argued and pleaded,
"Although our methods and tools are divergent,
we both want to probe the actuality of things
to investigate phenomena beyond their surfaces.
We have so much in common! For one thing,
we both use language to communicate."

But, retorted dainty Poetry,
"You follow the star of stern objectivity
while I prefer more intimate subjectivity,
you worship the goddess of reason
while I bend at the altar of intuition
concrete facts are all you have eyes for
while I dote on tangible essences.
Self is my universe and I am embarked
on a conquest of inner space.
No! Material and spirit will never mix!"
This put Science in rather a tight fix.

* *Shadkhan - Marriage Broker (in Hebrew).*

"The universe inside, and out, is our laboratory,"
he argued scientifically, sending Poetry flying.
"But I need you," he cried distractedly
"I can't live without you!"
Then Poetry in her flight arrested, turned,
"Is this a fact or an essence?" asked she.
"I don't know," he answered ruefully,
"Both, I think," he added truthfully.

Then smiling she gave him her hand,
and through the doors of perception
together they intuitively
and reasonably
danced.

Haim and Ada dancing through life.

MOUNT CARMEL POMEGRANATES

The trees smile, the trees laugh, the trees sigh,
and every pomegranate on Haifa's Mount Carmel
peals its love song:
take her tenderly by the hand
wherever you go,
she is part of you
we are witness.

The trees whisper,
the trees weep,
the trees sleep,
when he goes
and leaves her smile behind,
awakes at morning
in a snow land
kissing his own
cold hand.

Ada Aharoni

BROKEN WING

When she said
enough,
the happy flight in his eye
broke.
She could hear
the cracking of the bone,
shedding of white feathers
drooping on her flesh,
fraying the corners of her soul.

The engulfing of her hands
in his
did not bring back
the glimmer in the blue,
and one of the birds
in the dense, trembling wood,
the one with the happiest
longest whistle,
stopped
its song.

But the maiden with the green eyes
and dark lashes,
is not made to be a
breaker of wings,
she is made for song
and for laughter,
she yearns for the wings
to flap again in delight
in the blue –
without breaking
her own.

Ada Aharoni

DAVID AND BAT-SHEVA'S CAVE IN EIN GEDI

Silvery peach-colored clouds
Flowing in unending flock-row
Rippling through ice-cream skies,
Fusing, mellowing, melting,
Growing, flowing...

Fresh green baby leaf
Delicate transparent curves and dimples,
Softly fragile,
Waving being in the breeze,
Growing, flowing...

Resounding tear in the heart
Followed by another, and another,
Moist, spearlike,
As in dripping cave
On Ein Gedi's slippery cliff,
Where David and Bat-Sheva
Loved and hid –
Growing, flowing,
Submerging.

My beloved is unto me
as a cluster of camphire
in the vineyards of Ein Gedi

Song of Solomon 1:14

CLOUDED ALMOND FLOWERS

Your gaze was like almond flowers
on slopes of violet-patched
Biblical mountains

I touch it still
as my Jerusalem
over the amber horizon,
dancing cheek to cheek
"You are part of me."

But now,
with the rumble of guns
and suicide bombers
blowing up innocent
women and children,
the tune of your eyes
is again heavy-hearted,
gray clouding
our almond flowers

Tell me my love,
how can we
uncloak forever
the clouds
on our almond flowers?

Ada Aharoni

Twigs Not Roses

Your hand in my hair
planted twigs
not roses,
you whispered:
"there are no roses
around here
but you."

I kissed the
twig-bearing hand
as if it bore
all the crowns,
laurels
and pomegranates
in the land.

You are the garden
where I dream
full of trees, love and roses,
the lake where I bathe
among the beams of souvenirs.

In the heart of my mind
I again kiss
the twig-bearing hand
as if it bore
the finest ring
and richest chalet
in the land.

THE SLITS ON MY ARM

At the traffic light
of my life,
when you caressed my hair
and touched me
through the slits of my cherry shirt
with gentle silky finger,
as if there was a rose framed
in each small window on my arm –

I drank your sounds deep
of awakening roses,
light flowed sky blue
from your eyes
and flooded all
the shimmering tongues
at the source
of my being.

Ada Aharoni

One Way Journey

We have traveled deep,
there is no return.

Every bone
of your frame
has found its nook
in mine,
has caught
cannot let go.

Every turn of your chin
round mine
has pushed us farther
on the Carmel lane
of pomegranate exchange –
from which there is
no return.

No words,
no reason,
no facts,
no laws –
can stop our journey
now.

WILL TRANSPLANT

When you pressed
your heart
to mine
as if to sow it
under my ribs –

skin slipped
currents flowed
measure of muscle
to muscle

The surgery was
clean
and final –
our wills
transplanted.

Ada Aharoni

Psychological Wooing

I am glad
he does not love
with his tongue,
for his words
can dangle
forever
in my veins.

I am glad
he never tells me
he loves
my face
or my body,
like he loves
the sun, or good wine
or flowers.

I am glad...
then why
do I hear in me
tears dripping
like rusty leaves?

THE THREE GOWNS

I wore the gown
of laughter
and he smiled.

I wore the gown
of passion
and he frowned.

I wore the gown
of anger
and he fled.

Calmly
I re-adopted
the gown of
laughter
adorned with bright
distant jewels,
and he came back
nodding
a taste of pearl
moisture
on his lips.

But –
why does it not
satiate me?

Ada Aharoni

CHEST PROTEST

Interlocked deep,
curve of chest
in chest,
flesh protests against
apart
in human sounds –
like kissing knuckles

Cracking: you are part
of me.

Bone and muscle
know
what we do not fully
yet – that
there should be
no cleft.

YOUR NAME

Bells in hollows
peal your name continuously,
on artists' books,
on shop signs,
even on cans.

Landscapes stealthily
adopt your tones and colors,
conjuring your lithe deer walk,
secret charm.

The bells play mysterious
symphonies
transfusing your sounds
into blue space stars
running
to my heart.

They are pealing so
loudly
now my love,
can you too
hear them?

My beloved is like a roe
or a young hart:
behold, he standeth behind
our wall.
              Song of Solomon 2:9

37

Ada Aharoni

THE SWAN SEARCH

I looked for you
in the streets of Paris,
every swift, fawn-colored car
recalled your lithe limbs.

I looked for you in the King's garden
at Versailles,
rainbow-colored begonias conjured
the patterns of our rainbow moments.

I looked for you
in every Chateau of the Loire,
every white swan
gliding hopes on Lake Geneva,
every brown-roofed chalet
speckling the Alps became our nest.
I groped for the intensity of your agate eyes
in every mountain I encountered.

I looked for you everywhere,
but could only find you in me
everywhere,
in every urban
and suburban
cell of my
existence.

ISRAEL

To leave you now
would be an
amputation –
I would survive,
but
there would be
less
of
me.

Ada at Ramat Gader, near what used to be a Roman Bath

Interior Camera

Is the touring as long for you as for me?
Do you also meaningfully exist
only by the interior filming of me?

Far from the sunrise
of your eyes,
there is no picture my camera
cares to take or see.
This drifting among fragments
of city exposures, only develops
a thousand varieties of the source
of your smile.

Probing my skull's dark room,
I try to determine our position
in snaps black and white –
after this endless tour
there will be another
and another.

You stare beyond me at a loss,
accepting our present scanty shots,
while I, wide–eyed seek
further improved developments –
full length, real life
panoramic
pomegranate
love films.

Haim and Ada in Jordan mountains

YOUR REAL YOU

I do not fill my pen
with the moon dust
and green lawns of my mind
when I dwell upon you,
but in the limpid spring
of your real you
deep buried in your skin.

And the kind of tune I play
is not what I want to hear
as you maintain,
but the mysterious sounds you are.
The shapes of light I draw
are not from my own sun,
but from their source in you.

I look at you
not only with the tips of my hands,
but with wide-open eyes and ears.
It is not the idea of your smile
I love,
but your real smile
lingering on honey lips and teeth
I know cannot only kiss
but also bite.

So, if my pages
are wrapped with rainbows,
it is the astonishing effect
you had on me, you see,
when your barbed wires dropped,
and I saw the gentle spirit
hidden
in the tight-clasped fist.

Ada Aharoni

Four Mad Dogs

On our green path
they send four brown and black
mad dogs,
frantically barking fury,
leaping their convulsions at us,
their fangs frothing
billows of demented saliva
at our closeness.

But though with bloodshot eyes
they closely pursue,
they do not get
their prey.
We drive smoothly
through their clutches,
shut our windows,
enfold our arms tenderly
and cuddle
still closer.

They always send
four black and brown
mad dogs with pointed teeth,
when they smell what
they do not have –
but we will not let them
bite our
pomegranate
love.

Seaweed

*"The bombs are not the cause of the problem, but only the
symptoms of the deranged thought processes of man's mind..."*
        Helen Caldicott

I grapple with the edge
of the taste and shape of
nuclear bombs
like deadly rotten
mushroom.

You have kept your fears like an
underground river away from me,
preferred filling your pockets
with pebble-bombs
and seaweed silence.

You knew of my thirst
and river longings for –
yet not innovative enough to break away
from absurd deterrence reasoning
and send it flying.

My fears
refuse to stay in port,
they fling mushrooms and
brown seaweed like small
drowned hearts
full in my face.

Ada Aharoni

SILVER MOSAIC STONE

I give you this small
glowing stone with silver mosaic streaks,
chiselled from the sea of Galilee's breast.

When you curl your finger
around its permanence, remember –
the woman who gave it to me
was ready to give me her spring too,
but then
lethargy's manacles cried –
"We are not born free,
I am a slave,
young in years
but yet so old,
I feel eight hundred years old,
my will is buried with my father
under his bones in his grave."

"Is there then no hope for us?"
"Only after the flood."
 But Noah's flood was so long ago!
I am left with
silver streaks of
a mosaic stone
tying my tongue.
So I give you this silver streaked stone
full of me instead –
now lifeless
in your empty hand.

COMMON BLOODSTREAM

In one kind of fish the male attaches himself to the female
with his saber sharp teeth, eventually they share a common
bloodstream.
(Boston Aquarium)

You have strolled in me all year
all the length of my blue and red streams
until your folded lips
gently interlaced
the seams of my eyelids.

I once tried to filter you out
of my blood,
but you bit firmly
and wanted in.

Now you are so much me
my love –
I do not know anymore
what is me
what is you.

Ada Aharoni

FRAGILE

Part of me has left
to escape from you,
to grow whole again
like a smooth round melon,
after you dug English holes
in my pulp.

All of me is back –
I am almost whole again,
but lonely and need you.

This time my love,
remember I'm fragile,
please handle me
with care.

The stems that connect
my molecules to yours
are like those of thin
crystal wine glasses.

Be careful how you sip,
they break so easily.

HARD NUT

There is no scar
but only internal differences
where words seem to be written
with water ink
of unconvincing meanings.

There is no scar
but confusion of vision
in my hard-nut mind,
and yours –
each wrapped in
its own newspaper full of
infinite limited notions.

Yet, we still choose to drive on
together in the wind,
tumble in the same car,
kiss the same ear,
stroke same sand-dune back,
enter each other's curves,
each other's vision
each other's blindness,
we still choose to drive on
tenderly together
in the wind.

SUNFLOWERS

We did not know
We were two rooted
Sunflowers
With falling seeds –
Until
We tried
To move …

SILVER WEDDING RAINBOW IN NEW YORK CITY

You lifted me up high
waltzed me past our friends' smiles
seated at white tables
around the rainbow room,
round and round
around the rainbow room,
until I could almost touch
New York's blazing
messages all around.

"Put me down!" I cried,
laughing a silvery wedding laugh,
but you still whizzed me
round and round
higher than anybody
higher than the light.

"Is this what a silver wedding
is all about?" I laughed
a further bell laugh,
while some of our friends threw
wistful glances
at your silvery support of me
higher than anybody
higher than the light.

I kissed you joyously
my quarter of a century
silver-wedding-husband,
round and round
rainbow around.

51

Ada Aharoni

The End

I wonder
about the end of things.

My finger curls
around the root
of an essence:
when and where
our love will ever
cease to be the sap
I constantly breathe,
like a one time
glowing asphodel
fossilized into stone.

I dread whether a time
will come when your being
will cease to be
a Sabbath part of me,
when your hand
will cease
dissolving
into mine
like a honey bee
into a hyacinth,
when you
will just be you
and I
will just be me

like two lonely
rocks again
at the bottom
of the sea.

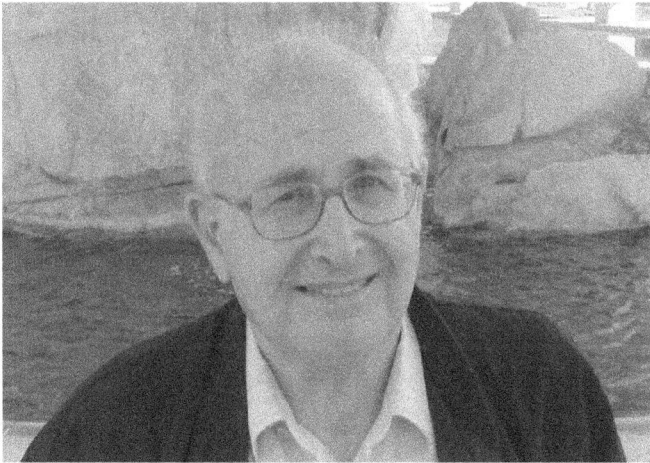

Haim in Los Angeles Museum

PART TWO

WOMEN POEMS

Contemplating a vision of peace and harmony
Picture of Ada in Jordan - taken by Haim Aharoni.

WOMAN OF NO TIME

I am the woman
Of no time

I envy those who have time
They envy me for having none.

My desire is to plant forests
But I only manage shrubs.

I want to run one million races
When I barely manage one!

Yet I know I'm not a fly
Born in the summer dawn
And dead in the afternoon,

My day is a pomegranate
Full of ruby grains –

Time must be my friend
Stopping me from tasting them all at once
So I can enjoy them one by one.

As long as each grain is a lifetime –
I do not care
If I'm the woman
Of no time.

MOTHERS YOU KNOW

*"We can best help you to prevent war not by repeating your words
and following your methods but by finding new words and creating
new methods."*
Virginia Woolf, Three Guineas

Mothers you know, a long time ago
have been wisely decreed
by diverse human creeds and needs –
goddesses of peace-in-the-home,
lavishly giving life, love and healing
through their wombs and life-blood.

And they have been quite successful
those loving peace-in-the-home mothers,
closely guarding us with their wisdom,
their tender words and watchful eyes.

Surely safer than in a Nuclear War
or in a new World War, or just a tiny war,
just the killing of one million or two –
so what about making mothers
the guardians of peace on earth?
Surely we wouldn't be so much worse?
And they are so available those mothers –
you can even find them in enemy land...

Look at the terrible mess they have
made of our blue planet, mother,
with atrocious terrorist bombers
blowing Twin Towers and blowing us!

You are the only one who can save us now,
mother, the only one who really knows
new words and new methods and can
create an innovative culture of peace to
protect your fearful children
weeping over their violent,
ailing world.

You are the only one who can heal
our blue planet, mother,
cradling it in your warm,
loving arms.

Ada Aharoni

You Cannot Bomb Me Anymore

Listen, little big man,
you cannot bomb me
anymore
because I don't allow you
to bomb me anymore
nor to choke
nor rape me anymore,
for I have my own strength now
and my own creative
peace business now

With this woman's mind
this woman's body
this woman's heart –
we don't allow you
to bomb us anymore –
for our sisters in Norway
have shown us the way
and now –
you cannot bomb us
anymore!

For it is
the grandmother
who will do away with
the big bad wolf – War,
and not the other way round!

We global women
will all join hands
and banish the big bad
War Wolf
from our lives.

And you will not be able
to bomb us, bomb us,
ANYMORE.

Ada Aharoni

PEACE IS A WOMAN AND A MOTHER

How do you know
peace is a woman?
I know, for I met her yesterday
on my winding way
to the world's fare.
She had such a sorrowful face
just like a golden flower faded
before her prime.

I asked her why
she was so sad?
She told me her baby
was killed in Auschwitz,
her daughter in Hiroshima
and her sons in Vietnam, India, Pakistan,
Ireland, Israel, Palestine, Lebanon,
Bosnia, Rwanda and Chechnya.

All the rest of her children, she said,
are on the nuclear
black-list of the dead,
all the rest, unless –
the whole world understands
that Peace is a Woman

A thousand candles then lit
in her starry eyes, and I saw –
Peace is indeed a pregnant woman,
Peace is a mother.

TEDDY BEARS FOR GUNS

My man of the year
Is the wonderful, wise one
Who sat himself in the midst
Of the West with a huge box
Of chubby Teddy Bears
On New Year's Eve
Of the third millennium
Attracting an endless
Queue of cheering kids –
Holding guns

He playfully showed
With a smile and a wink
And a Teddy Bear hug –
It could be the beginning
Of a honey-laden decade
In a brave new world

By wisely trading
Guns
For Teddy Bears.

Ada Aharoni

THE MORE INTERESTING LIFE

Come closer sisters
hear the man
and what he sang about us.

At twelve, a sharp bayonet fear
jabbing through my ribs
tickled my mind:
You are a male,
you will have to go to war,
you may be killed!

Shrieking shells
and giant mushrooms flying
filled my blazing night falls.
I looked at the lively girls, envy nibbling,
they will not go to war,
they will not be killed.

But suddenly a flash –
a vision of kitchen sinks
a life of drying dishes
and of soiled diapers.

The bayonet externalized,
I held it with firm fist
and nodded reassured:
"But I shall have
the more interesting life."

That's it sisters, that's what he sang,
what he sang about us.

What do we do now with what he sang,
What he sang about us?
Let us all loudly sing our own harmonious songs and together
change the heart of
the melody
of his song.

Prof. Edwin David Diday, Ada's brother, with her in Paris.

A Bridge of Peace

*"They shall sit every man under his vine and under his fig tree,
and none shall make them afraid."*
                (The Bible, Micah, 4, 4).

"He who walks in peace - Walk with him!"
                (The Koran - Sura 48)

My Arab sister,
Let us build a sturdy bridge
From your olive world to mine,
From my orange world to yours,
Above the boiling pain
Of acid rain prejudice –
And hold humane hands high
Full of free stars
Of twinkling peace.

I do not want to be your oppressor
You do not want to be my oppressor,
Or your jailer
Or my jailer,
We do not want to make each other afraid
Under our vines
And under our fig trees blossoming
On a silvered horizon above the
Bruising and the bleeding of
Poisoned gases and scuds.

So, my Arab sister,
Let us build a sturdy bridge of
Jasmine understanding
Where each shall sit with her baby
Under her vine and under her fig tree –
And none shall make them afraid
AND NONE SHALL MAKE THEM AFRAID.

Ada with Arab Women of IFLAC - the Bridge

Ada Aharoni

Cosmic Woman

They tell us you were first born
in warm ocean womb
caressed by sun fingers –
daughter perhaps
of the stormy love
of two unruly atoms
maddened by the solitude
of eternal rounds
in the steppes of times.

And your children,
lively descendants
of their stellar nucleus mother
dropped from the sky
in depths of ocean belly,
born of green and brown seaweed
and the laughs and cries
of blue bacteria.

Cosmic woman,
when you chose earth
as home for your vast roots
at the beginning
of the great human family,
it was for life –
not for death.

Cosmic woman,
you, who were born of the nucleus,
from deadly nuclear mushroom
Save your children
SAVE YOUR CHILDREN.

Ada Aharoni

Assa and Farah of Isfahan

"Wherever I am,
Farah likes it"
Assa announced
At the Tea-House Khane
With bubbling male pride,
His young beard and tongue husky,
His eyes gleaming in the 'gaz'
nougat-nut atmosphere
of a Persian miniature.

Farah nodded a violet nod,
while her brown chestnut hair
became a shade sadder
against the giant copper kettles,
and through the notes
of 'Hey Hoda!' – 'Oh my God!'
she whispered in my ear:
"You look happy,
I do not know
many happy women."

Isfahan, Iran, 1976

RABBI GERSHOM

I was a bandaged female in an ancient ark
When Rabbi Gershom came and saved me,
killing the dragon of polygamy
who was strangling me
far back in the tenth century –
giving me the right to say:
nay – I want to be
just one wife not one
among four.

Where are the Rabbi Gershom of today?
Oh where are they?
For ten centuries I have been waiting
in this stifling museum
for my equal right to be
a witness, to testify,
to be a Judge,
like Biblical Deborah.

But no more - I'm alive and awake
not a bandaged Golem* anymore
not a slave, not a child –
time to untie custom bandages
grown musty and choking.

Time to open my ark wide
and freely tread the earth
in search of ripe
equal pomegranates.

Golem: Dummy, idiot.

Ada Aharoni

A Ladino Song in Toledo

Again, and again I am there in the West –
though I am here in the East –
there in that *Aranjues* wine-cellar tunnel in Toledo,
winding towards the river.

Since that mustached shop-owner showed me
an ancient eight-branched Menorah* he found
in his cave, dropped by my ancestors, fleeing
the wolves' teeth of the Inquisition –
I am still breathlessly running
in the tunnel, tightly holding the Menorah -
there in Toledo,
though I am here.

In that café in front of the synagogue
which has been turned into Maria Bianca's church,
a singer, named Ada, like me,
with deep "fatho" voice
sang to my soul a Ladino song,
my grandmother sang to me:
El pasharo se vola el Korasson Yora
Yora mi alma yora, no te deshan vivir,
tenemos mala gentes,
no te deshan vivir ...
"The bird flies, the heart cries,
weep my soul weep,
for there are bad people
who do not let us live…"

Menorah: candelabrum, lamp.

72

A shiver ran down my spine
sending me flying breathlessly
still holding the
Menorah tightly in my arms –

I am still there running in the West
though I'm already here
in Israel
in the East.

Ada Aharoni

Abishag's Secret

What Abishag thought,
blossoming fifteen-year old lying taut
wide-eyed on kingly bed silent
at the side of old King David, probably was –
"What bad breath the old King has!"

Father bade me hold my tongue and go
to the King in Jerusalem.
Mother wiped my tears with soft words,
said I should be proud to be the chosen one
among all the beauties of the land
to warm royal bones –
but they didn't tell me
what bad breath King David has!

His handmaids taught me how to caress and revive him
his courtiers showed me how to give life,
so that they could keep rivals at bay.
They decorated me queen-bride, fragrant like a rose,
brought me trembling to the royal bed,
but I can't smile, can't touch –

The poor King smells like the carcass
of the once beloved horse
in our neighbor's field in Shunem.
Before it died, the farmer covered his horse
with a sack to warm his bones back to life –
but the vultures came anyway.

I am the courtiers' sack
to keep the vultures away.
But oh God! What bad smell King David has!
It smothers me, it chokes me, his breath,
mother, it strangles me!
Oh mama, come and save me,
I shall die, oh God!
What misery, what a tragedy,
what should I do?

I left the bed,
I left the kingly room,
I ran away and hid in the shed,
bathed in flowing tears.

In the morning, just after golden dawn,
Great King David was no more,
and I was no more queen,
just a poor little girl from Shunem
weeping bitter tears for
having failed
to give life
to a King.

A Jewish Woman's Prayer

Bless you, oh Lord
for having made me a woman,
for if you had made me a man
I would have had to pray:
"Bless you Oh Lord
for not having
made me
a woman!"

Ada in Nepal (1982)

LIVING GODDESS IN NEPAL

Pretty ten-year old
little girl
a full-fledged goddess
at the foot of the Himalaya

Wooden palace
and crowned head
earrings and make-up
cannot hide your sad smile
and dazed eyes
at the foot of the Himalaya

For you know
the day would soon come
when your menstrual blood
will freely flow
and chase you
from your queenly palace
at the foot of the Himalaya

A goddess no more
you will descend again
among humans
once more
who will praise you no more,
for you will become just
a frightened little girl
an ex-Goddess who
has lost her childhood –
at the bottom of the Himalaya.

Katmandu, Nepal, 1982

Ada standing by the painting she painted titled:
THINKING WOMAN.

Not In Your Museum Anymore

On the Liberation of Woman at the Opening of the
Third Millennium

Embalmed in your
Mummifying caresses I
Was a zombie
A bandaged mummy
In an ancient sarcophagus
Patiently waiting centuries
For you to open the lid
When you could spare the time.

But no more,
I am alive –
Not a zombie
Not a mummy anymore,
Time to untie sterile bandages
Grown musty,
Time to open the lid wide
And tread the earth freely
In search of rolling
Pomegranates.

I don't belong
To your museum
Anymore.

Ada Aharoni

Las Manianitas

Dedicated to Mexican Elia Domenzain

You are yourself dear Elia
One of those flashing black–eyed manianitas
Sung by King David, in your moving
Birthday song!

What a surprise to hear my grandmother
Regina's Ladino cradle song
Crowned national Mexican Birthday Anthem,
Sung by cheerful Maryachi in quaint artist cafe
And in colorful, melodious Garibaldi Square –
In Mexico City!

Did the Marranos bring the song over
The frothy oceanic waves
When they fled
From the devouring teeth of Spain's Inquisition,
To the redeeming, blazing sun of
Mexico City and Monterrey?

Despertia! You taught us,
"Me bien despierta" – Wake up!
And we woke up wide-eyed
To the rich beauty and tragedy of historic
And present-day Mexico, flashing
Through your blazing eyes and
Palpitating red lips.

You shared with us the secret beauty of
Frida Kahlo's dramatic paintings in her
Own home, now turned into a museum.
Her amazing colorful mystical message
Now flows smoothly in my own veins
Whispering urgently *"Despertia..."*

Beautiful, graceful *Manianita* friend,
Your poignant love of peace culture
Perfumed with deep rose Aztec flowers
And gilded incense, poems and plays,
Have richly embaumed
My life.

Mexican Amanecio

*"Every gun that is made, every warship launched, every rocket
fired signifies, in the final sense, a theft from those who hunger and
are not fed, those who are cold and are not clothed."*
        Dwight D. Eisenhower

Mexico has "Amanecio" - has arisen
and has woken me up, with her true story
of the rising sun filled with night memories
of her tragic conquered Indian past
which has filled my inner world
with powerful Aztec sun Gods
and steep Mayan Pyramids.

In the present, her life-force
still bears the scars of her conquered past
in the shaded dark eyes
of her poor, barefoot children
kissed tenderly by warm mothers,
before they are sent to sell fake pearl necklaces
and illuminated paintings
of rich Mexican landscapes
in flashing orange and golden colors.

I now wear Mexico's dainty pearl necklace
around my tourist throat
woven by a little Manianita with pearly eyes.
"Mire que ya amanecio!"
flashed her triumphant smile,
when she succeeded to sell her pearls
to me on the bus.
The sun rose again in her eyes,
crowned by her mother's kiss and hug.

Mexico, your *hacienda* kindness,
Your warm vivacity, your awakening energy –
Has filled me with hope
That our world at the end of the twentieth
"Mushroom Century" will at long last fully
Lavish food and education - not arms,
On all the hungry children of our world.

Global Village –
Your turn to fully *"Amanecio!"*

Written at the XIV World Congress of Poets,
Monterrey and Mexico City, August 1993

Ada Aharoni

THE POOR

All The Poor With Plenty Fed

Is Dryden's Mirabilis dream –
"All the poor with plenty fed,"
Reachable at last in our own fat days?

Mother, oh mother I'm so hungry
I have sharp-toothed rats in my stomach!

What would it take today
For all the poor to be plenty fed?
Should the rich grab less and let
Some juicy morsels fall
Into the laps of hungry children?

Mother, oh mother I'm so hungry
I have sharp-toothed rats in my stomach!

Should bank managers get only
Three times more salary than their staff
And not a hundred times more?

When will governments understand
That it is nobler and more just
To feed the poor than to
Feed their guns with deathly bullets
And their tanks and airplanes with shells,
Napalm and rockets?

Mother, oh mother I'm so hungry
I have sharp-toothed rats in my stomach!

Can the dream come true today?
Don't be a Don Quixote!
The rich will go on being richer
The poor will go on being poorer
And hungry children will go on dreaming
Of delicious banquets when they go to sleep
On craving empty stomachs.

Mother, oh mother I'm so hungry
I have sharp-toothed rats
In my stomach and in my belly!

Loss of the Milky Way

In the land of milk and honey,
milk shut me out forever.
My doctor calls it allergy
and I call it tragedy.
Your enzyme for that one
is dead, he kindly explains.

But how did it die? I protest in dismay,
I love milk so
with mounts of choco
ice-cream and cake, cheeses and butter,
I desperately mutter.
You may truly love milk, the doctor nods,
but it surely does not love you!

I mourn and bid goodbye to my Milky–Way
and staunchly climb my dry winding path.

Though all my land has emptied of milk –
I will try to fill it with honey!

Daughter of Sinai

They have come again with their washed faces
And their green and yellow bags full of goodies,
But not for me little Sulha of the desert
Nor for my three greedy brothers.

"Toda raba"* is a magic word
For opening those bright treasure bags
From which we get biscuits and sweets,
Meat, coins, smiles and frowns.

This one looks at me demandingly,
I shall not let her take my picture
Unless she pays me the required snap-money,
I cannot squander my image so.

My black eyes dart furtive looks,
My mouth curls in defiance.
I hide behind my burly brothers
And shout the silent noise of the desert.

They are all gone, swallowed
by their big blue giant camel,
Those strange creatures from beyond the desert.
Could I just once find their nylon bags' spring
I would bring back piles and piles, numberless
As the sands of the desert.

* *Toda raba: many thanks (in Hebrew).*

Massada

I was at Segera, Golda said,
With a historic look
Two thousand years old,
Flickering from her wan, freckled face,
Each freckle a wrinkle of wisdom –
I was at Ein Gedi too,
And I had to come back home to
Massada.

I looked at her aged booted figure,
A disquiet feeling nibbling,
Could she make it?
She was so much part of it
Yet so out of place,
With her burden of four score
And her frail, frail Itsik
Wobbling stoically behind her,
To Massada.

"I was often here before…"
Her voice had the sound of the mountain.
"You young people do not understand,
You cannot understand the meaning of coming back –
I had to come back as before,
Two thousand years ago - before I go."
She then embraced the tortuous snake climb,
Each heavy tread bringing her closer up
To Massada.

I felt guilty for letting them continue
That which might shorten their days.
She was nothing to me – I was nothing to her,
Then why this gnawing feeling for this mounting rock
That would not abide?
I argued, and offered my hand, but to no avail.
The winds flapped the gates of Golda's ancient memory,
And she generously offered me the insight of her eighties.
At the center I read –
Massada.

I turned my back on the aged couple, in despair,
My feet doubly aching, for me and for them.
At the top of Massada, I had no more wish
To inhale the mystery of Herod's ruins,
Than to find out
What had become of the aged couple.
Had physical weakness overcome will-power, this time?
Had they collapsed on the way like desert rocks,
Joining Massada?

Then suddenly Golda surged from the brown cliffs,
A triumphant white apparition.
An exuberant look of sublime joy
Illuminated her old, old face
In a radiant way I shall never forget.
Then, I knew it was wrong of me
To have tried to stop them.
Ancient mute cries flashed in her triumphant eyes:
"We have come back home!
Massada will never fall again..."

ARTURO'S RUBINSTEIN

"The power of Creation seems to favor human beings who love life
unconditionally, and I am certainly one who does..."
Arthur Rubinstein

Today you are ninety Arturo,
and you play us your Rubinstein
fingers lovingly enlacing
life's hidden allegro
"Every day is the happiest
one for me,
living an intensive life
is my secret –
I've never met a person
as joyful as me!"

My friends wink and say,
"Perhaps that's because
he's never met you!"

I'm not sure they're right,
then I think of your dazzling smile
my love, suffusing my sky with symphonies
like fresh rain on scorched earth.

I dance with the joyous waves of life,
sunbeams of the Garden of Eden on earth,
like my Internet that causes me to sing:
"I have the whole wide world in my hand..."
And am filled with –
So glad to meet you,
Dear Mr. Rubinstein!

Papyrus Fan

I decline the honor of being
Your impeccable sabi anymore,
To wobble gently, obediently,
In your footsteps,
With painted face
And high-heeled shoes,
Holding the luscious papyrus fan
High up to your ego.

The heat is as stifling
For me, as for you,
And the fan whispers
The same promises to me
As to you –
So what about holding it
Up to me
For a change?

Or still preferably –
It is so heavy anyway,
What about holding it
Together?

Ada Aharoni

Mimosa Flowers

I wait for the day
blossoming as a mimosa,
when half the world's presidents
will be women
with arms flowing cosily
around every child's cry –
Shalom.

And the sun will shine
on all mortals
with equal golden rays
in every green field,
every printed book
every human look –
Shalom.

Sister Etty with Ada

DAPHNE

I did not know
Bernini's Daphne
was in my own Carmel woods!

I discovered her
one mysterious moist afternoon
poised on legend green
stillness.

Her face
a flower in curved sorrow
tilted backwards,
flowing shoots
fanned the earth,
while leafy arm-branches
raised up twig-tips
in veined supplication
towards the sky.

Daphne
blowed anguished seeds
of yearning
for the freedom she
and we were meant to have
germinating
in my own soul.

I grow roots in
Daphne's
soil.

Ada Aharoni

Love Games

Sorry, I took it seriously.
I put you at the very top
of the ladder, up there with my breath
and the sun –
but did not get warm.

For you, I was lying somewhere
in the middle rungs
with movies and games
you play once a week
then brush aside
when something more important sprouts.
No need to worry about games,
They're always there in the cupboard
waiting breathlessly
for the playboy
to open the door.

But no more –
I have adjusted my scales
to fit yours,
and am ready for the game.
And anyway,
games are so much more fun...

Be careful,
I've started to play.

CRUMPLED CURTAIN

Our lovely curtain
is all sadly crumpled again,
its flowered folds painfully
jerking one another
in silent protest,
sticking its frayed angles
like protruding nerves
in a heap.

You have again pushed it
back callously,
with stout unfeeling fingers,
disturbed its smooth flowing harmony,
one fold after another
painfully crying out its
ruffled protest and testimony –

This is what
you unfeelingly sometimes do
to my feelings.

Free Lioness Queen

Recoiling over wound,
From biting teeth of wars
Choking,
As if she had gobbled smoldering coal –
The lioness paces, plots,
Thunders –
Then erupts in full glory
Air-poised paw
Mane aglow,
Full queen of her dazzling
World again.

Climbing majestically on her throne
In all her auburn splendour,
She gazes around superb
At her numerous
Hungry subjects.

Queenly, shaggy head raised
Amber eyes shooting,
She roars her mighty royal paean
High up into the deafness of mute sky,
Then pulls it like a carpet,
And briskly shakes its stars
And Horn of Plenty
All over our hungry
Global Village.

Upright

I gazed enraptured
At the tide of children
circling gaily and waving limbs
To the beat of a tambourine.

"Choose your gestures,"
The teacher's voice
Floated loud and clear
Above the barefoot din.

As by magic,
The children divided
Into those with bent backs
And those who crawled on fours.

Except for the odd one
Who stood his ground,
Looked to the left, looked to the right,
And preferred to remain
Upright.

Ada Aharoni

CHAMELEON

You raise your voice and cry –
till when will you agree
till tomorrow morning?
You see me
as a chameleon with rolling eyes
who changes its skin color
at the touch of your voice,
then goes back to
ignorant insipid colors
on other lethargic
backgrounds.

You want to reveal
your world of ideas
before my fractured chameleon eyes,
to cut through my wrapped vision
with your translucent truths
thrown at me like crystal balls,
and you rage
when I do not
pick them up.

But I'm not a chameleon,
I'm me, your partner.
And when I agree,
it is only to the nuances
of some of the angles
of your words.

Not to all their colors
not all their reflections.
I have my own colors
my own reflections
rooted in me
as deeply
as yours.

When I try
to present a new perception
before your clouded eyes,
I don't consider them blind.
You have a right to your
crystal balls
as I to mine.

My darling,
they have already cut down
our Daphne tree,
don't let us
continue their cutting job.
Let's help each other
love each other
despite our different colors,
not hurt each other.

I'm not a chameleon,
you're not a chameleon –
we're equal loving friends
and faithful partners.

Ada Aharoni

Not Even On Her Birthday

One buzz on.
They said they would take her out
to birthday-dance,
this time they sounded they really meant it,
could not possibly postpone.

Two buzzes, off.
They jammed her birthday tears deep in her throat,
throttled her slotted expectancy,
callously tore up her birthday road
with careless words.

Three buzzes on off.
Did she imagine for one
smiling-moon moment
she could keep her bliss intact?
Forty four years
forty four buzzes off, off, off.

She lay livid in white sheets
her liver swollen
to once and a half its normal size,
while future years
waltzed away like flowing sand
through her numb groping fingers,
buzz after buzz, after buzz,
all merely buzzes.

She did not believe them anymore.
Would never be caught
in their buzz-traps again.
Last buzz off.

Ada Aharoni

GEISHA GIRLS

Hai, squid and seaweed in bamboo boat.
Mother, what is she doing to my husband,
rubbing his chest and leg and ego?
Hai, jelly fish and seaweed in roasted eye.

Mother, why did you tell me
they are just psychological hostesses
sometimes singers and dancers,
but nothing more?

If a psychologist caressed my breast and leg
wouldn't Kikuji be annoyed too?
And when I need a psychologist, mother,
whom do I go to?

Hai, crab and seaweed in parching mouth,
which unlike yours and granny's
refuses to be custom-choked.

Mother, oh mother, I'm so lonely when he goes
to the geisha girls.

I dangle a thousand million cranes for the day
when the geishas will rise from the tatami
in their rose-winged kimonos
mount the bamboo boat
and float –
straight out
of our lives.

Hokkaido, Japan, July 1976

SHANI

Golden-ginger curls,
peach fists in incubator
holding year two thousand in one,
and us in the other.

Tiny Shani
promising as the bright scarlet light
in the horizon over the sea,
you will be twenty three springs
in the twenty first century.

How will our world then be?
United, warless?
Every tear wiped
in every hungry eye?
Equal opportunities for you
as for him?

You calmly lie in your
jeans-colored uni-sex perambulator
smiling your mother's smile
enveloped in your father's glee,
and wave a tiny arm
reassuringly.

How come I already
love you so
Shani?

21 February, 1977

Ada Aharoni

Grandmother and the Wolf

In memory of Ebba Haslund, my friend from Norway

She looked at me with wise
bluebell eyes
and told me the brothers Grimm
had it all wrong,
they had it all wrong, you see,
for it was the grandmother
who gobbled up the big bad wolf
and not the other way round.

They were too grim,
those brothers Grimm,
and they had it all wrong –
for grandmothers you see,
are very strong!

Ada's Grandmother Regina

PART THREE

A GARLAND OF GRAIN

SON ON HIS OWN

Twenty
years ago
as if yesterday,
your baby forehead –

Puck!
bumped into mine
seriously in play.

Today,
in your honey beard son,
you have gone to a home of your
own
a mate of your own,
you stand beyond me
straight and handsome,
and distant

As if I had given birth
to a smiling traveling
bearded butterfly
intent on his way –

May it always be one of
creativity, joy
and love.
my son.

Ada with granddaughter Shani

BABY SHANI'S SMILE ON MOUNT CARMEL

Redhead Shani,
Like a russet sun rising
Under cloudy pines
Under needles
Among cones –
Smiled to me today
A honey and milk smile
Sculpting my flesh
With dewy eyes.

Little pink flower toes
In light blue overall
Skip the air
Hands praising, staccato,
Like a fairy baby maestro
Waving invisible wands
Feasting my look.

Tiny Shani smiled –
And all the world opened,
All the trees, all the cones,
All the flowers, all the needles –
All the world smiled back
Driving away the pine clouds in me,
Nodding with wondering dewy eyes –
Yes, yes, all is
Yes.

15 Sept. 1977

Ada Aharoni

IDAN AND THE WAVES

The three year-old opened
his big blue eyes,
the color of the sea –
and gazed with wonder at the waves
and then at me,
sitting on a rock in Bat-Galim
the Daughter of the Sea –

Why do the waves run away,
run away, all the time,
away, away from me?
And where do they go
when they run faraway,
faraway, all the time
away from me?

Dear Idan, it is not away from you
but back to where they belong.

Even then, like now,
your curious brain thirstily
tried to seize the flitting essence
of the waves of life,
of retreat of advance.

Even then like now,
your big blue eyes,
the color of the sea,
tried to grasp the ungraspable
about the hidden secrets
in frothy bubble waves
in our turbulent, unpredictable
inner and outer sea.

Dear Idan,
may you always succeed
to grasp the essence
of waves of kindness
and of sunbeams
of advance.

FROM GRANDFATHER PAPOU TO GRANDSON IDAN

My Papou,
Good news on the tail of the wind,
Your granddaughter's grandson
With cute Beatle hairstyle –
Like you, is born in Israel too.
A mount of Mazal Tov papou,
Wherever you are.

You, born in nineteenth century Jaffa,
Wandering among the nations
On the dangerous Medusa raft,
Three generations on the Nile,
Then the flowing Seine
And domed Milan.

Your idealistic granddaughter
Back to Israel –
And now Idan, papou,
Idan is here
Closing the five generations
Cycle roots
From Jaffa to Haifa.

This time papou,
Not with a ribboned box
Of Cairo's Groppi
Melting fondant sweets
With walnuts tasting of evanescence,
But with almond kernels
In strong shells,
Roots planted here
In the promised land -

This time for good,
For good, papou.

THE SECOND EXODUS

Today, I again bring my grain vessel
to the docks of your granary, father –
while breathing the wheat smells you loved,
me in Dagon Silo in Haifa,
you far away back in Cairo.

Joseph in Egypt land, Canaanite jugs,
ritual bronze sickles from temples,
crushing-stones, mill-stones and mortars –
all link me back to you.

I remember your orange-beige office
in Cairo's Mouski,
with deaf Tohami weighing
the heavy sacks of flour and grain
on old rusty scales,
and me listening unaware
to the birds' chirped warning
on the beams of your ceiling:
"Wandering Jew, open your Jewish eyes,
you will soon have to spread your wings
again, and look for a new nest."

Mighty Dagon's giant arms storing in bulk,
fill my own silo with tears
that you are not here with me
to view this wonder
deftly handling bread to Israel -
the land you so loved
but are not buried in.

For you dear father,
I plant today a garden of grain,
for you, who always taught us
how to sow.

MAMICA

You read Rousseau's "Emile",
yet knew it instinctively
by heart.
Let us roam barefoot
in golden fields of home,
sleep with open windows wide

Gave us all you had
with two full hands
of bedstead copper angels.
Sometimes you forgot to eat,
but never to feed us.
Whatever we did or said
was a diamond mine –
you children were your little gods.

Even when I left you and France
for a country I loved,
you were not hurt nor angry,
gave your daughter
to the kibbutz in Israel
with a smile followed by a tear.

Today we worship you in return,
Mamica*, like a queen emerging
from Paris metro's belly,
to Bat-Galim, daughter of the waves,
queen of the waves again
as in Alexandria –
mother, mamica, standing on a shell
crowned by love.

'Mamica' is an endearment for 'mother' in Ladino.

Family at Versailles
Haim, Ginette, Ada, Pierre and mamica Fortunee (Fifi)

Ada Aharoni

A GREEN WEEK

A week like fresh mint,
a green week spreading
its fragrance to the roots
of my being.

"Have a green week!"
My father used to bless us
on Saturday nights in Cairo,
when he came back
from the "Gates of Heaven"
the Grand Synagogue
in Adli Street.

"Have a green week"
he beamed,
brandishing a fresh,
fragrant mint branch
over our curly heads –
but don't keep that green week
only to yourselves -
give it back
to the world
fully blossoming.

Who will give me
a green week
now that he's gone?
Now that the Gates of Heaven
are shut?

Only peace –
only a fragrant
mint peace.

Fortunee with daughters Ada and Ginette in Paris

Ada, with Mother Fortunée in Los Angeles park

DEAR DESCARTES: CREATIVITY

Dear Descartes,
Not only "I think, therefore I am,"
but mostly –
      I create, therefore I am.

I am me for having given birth
to my poetas, my creations,
my children,
my feelings
      and not only my thoughts.

I gaze intently at my offspring,
my creation, my oeuvre,
launched for life –
vibrating sharp soft sparks
of magnetic birth and growth,
marvelously quenching my desire
and thirst –
pure essence
      of sheer vitality

Not only I think, but mostly –
I create –
therefore
I am!

REGINA

The saving of Jews by Turkey during the Spanish Inquisition

In Toledo, 520 years ago my great, great,
great grandmother Regina,
fleeing the Inquisition's torture wheels
poured her Spanish tears into velvet black veil
and sailed over the crimson waves
with thousands of sisters and brothers
to Izmir, to Izmir.

She had to leave behind her beloved illuminated poems,
her ancient Bible and painted Haggada,
her illustrious father's
celebrated scientific parchments -
her whole Spanish Golden Age
as she sailed with the stars
on sad purple waves
to Izmir, to Izmir.

The bird stopped flying
the heart stopped crying
as it preened its traumatic feathers
and nestled cozily on quaint warm roofs
in the new Turkish mosaic haven
lavished by filigree hospitality
sheltering a new hope in Regina's amber eyes,
on the azure, silvery shores of
Izmir.

Suddenly Regina's beautiful, noble figure
stands majestically before me
whispering a Ladino message:
"What we should be celebrating today
is the saving of a quarter of a million
of our brothers and sisters
more than 520 years ago by Turkey,
and not only the reconciliation with Spain..."
I listen closely and nod.

Now Regina smiles again
and flies to the wide open gates of
Upper
Golden Jerusalem.

Ada Aharoni

GRAFFITI UNDER THE TABLE

I turned our kitchen table
upside down
to paint its legs white,
on its belly
scribbled in red oil crayon,
babyish letters glared
"Ariel is a good boy."

His quaint graffiti
tear-blurted
on the inner screen
wistfully protested
self-preservation,
probably against me –
for having scolded him
for not washing
his chubby fingers,
or not eating fish
or spinach.

The plump red words
staunchly stood
beneath the table
on the hidden screen
braving the years,
as love stands
on a slapped face

slapping mine
across the years.

Talia and her Brother Ariel

Time in Abadan: Homage to Omar Khayyam

Life is but a checkerboard of nights and days
Which Destiny for pieces plays.
He moves, he mates, he slays
And one by one
Back in the box he lays
          Omar Khayyam, Rubayat

In green, peaceful Abadan,
the long longed-for treasure
flowed profusely into my lap,
fluid more precious
than its black gold –
the pure transparent gold
of Time.

Time to think what Omar
really meant when he wrote:
"While you live
Drink!
For once dead
you never shall return."
Time, like him,
to adjourn to this "earthen bowl"
under two shady palm trees,
"My lips the secret well of life to learn."

Time to mark the remarkable lines
with a jasmine exclamation,
and slip a Persian miniature
on their depth.

Time to open my long arms wide,
and perform the unique feat
of listening closely to my pulse –
and wonder how steadily
forward its pace is!

Mother and Daughter Closeness
Talia and Ada in Abadan (Iran, 1976)

ABDUL'S CHILDREN

Abdul's Children
Will not know more
Than Abdul does,
for Abdul's children
Are not taught more
Than Abdul was.

Benevolent Ladies –
Stuff your ears
With cocktail parties
Your noses with caviar,
With Champagne your eyes –
Then no more sighs,
You will not hear
Nor smell nor see
Their illiterate cries.

Abadan, Iran, 1976

In Memory of My Uncle Jacques

Bohemian laughter and moustache
Mustard tan, mustered life
with one arm.
Villa in flowered Doki
with monkey and pool,
tropical golden fish.

Dark musty hole in Paris
crowning six creaky flights.
Broad jokes crackled
next to the stove – on the stove
coffee and magnitude.

Life is a hoax
my Uncle Jacques laughingly confided,
roam it in open car with or without
coin or hole in pocket,
from Green Island to Rome
before you leave home.

With one arm – not one leg.
The bubble of life
burst with the leg –
he roams no more.

But warm laughter
and chuckled joke
ring and roam.

Ada Aharoni

SAUL BELLOW: PLEASE GET OUT FROM UNDER MY PILLOW

Dear Saul Bellow,
please get out from under
the existentialist creases of my pillow,
where you have been lurking
these past five years.

Praise you,
for having strengthened me
in brushing aside the Doom Sayers
with their pipsqueak religions
of void and gloom –
for your wise words
clinging like ripe peaches
to my cells

But now,
please move from under my pillow,
for I'm a freed prisoner
of my Ph.D.
The time has at last come
for me to pass my own words along,
to try myself to
"Seize the Day,"
instead of merely analyzing yours.

At my crossroad, I send you
a library of thanks
Nobel Saul Bellow
for having been my close
and staunch, learned companion
these five full
Rain King years.

But now, dear Saul Bellow,
please get out from under
my pillow, and let me be
me!

Ada Aharoni and Nobel Laureate Saul Bellow at the
International Saul Bellow Conference Ada organized
at Haifa University (1988)

Not Old: Saul Bellow Indeed Knew

Even Mr. Sammler
that one-eyed septuagenarian
was not too old to be involved
in his planet

    "But I feel a hundred years old"

You young mensch who have saved
your eye from the oven
have a full store of ripe pomegranates
if you only care to pick them up

    "But I feel a hundred years..."

Why can you only carry
the heavy public banner
and not your precious
private loved one?

    "But I feel a hundred..."

Remember what Ramona said to Herzog?
"An old man smells old,
your smell is young"

"But I feel..."

A woman can also tell
about love, about life,
from the spring of a sunrise smile
in deep blue eyes
like violets on Mount Carmel,
and the breath of a caress
like a flaming russet bush.

"I feel Saul Bellow indeed knew."

The Roger Dance

The Roger dance is not over,
when you dance this way -
it's forever.

Graceful, elegant steps,
charm and majestic poise
legs nimble, stretched
arms curved, yearning to grasp
the bizarre whims of life
and strange humanity.

With a knowing, tender, witty, wistful smile
you lead your dancing partner
into your enchanted world
where cardboard becomes gold
where hatred becomes harmony.

They told me Roger, like Heraclitus,
"they told me you were dead
they brought me bitter news to hear
and bitter tears to shed,
I wept as I remembered
how often you and I had tired the sun..." (1)
with dancing, and sent him down the sky

For when you dance this way through life,
through wonderful poems,
dear Roger –
it is forever.

*(1) The lines in quotation marks are from Tennyson's poem
on the death of Roman Heraclitus. In addition to his being
a great poet, Roger, who was a peace-loving Bahai, was a
member of a ballet company and appeared on Canadian
Television. He was a member of the Poetry Group VOICES
ISRAEL. He died from cancer, in 1994.*

THE SNAKE ON THE WATERMELON SKIN

My sea bound leg through the ladder window
Was suddenly pinned to mid air by
The piercing pin-glitter of
A beady charcoal eye!
In Camp Caesar,
Under Alexandria's blue skies
A hieroglyphic presence
On a watermelon skin
crippled me in the paralyzed stillness.

I did not cry, I did not recoil, but gaped transfixed
Afraid to tremble, lest I disturb the mystery of our silent tryst.
He watched from every brown loop of his long, lithe body
While his face breathed back on me breath for breath
Overpowering my frozen blood.

Then I knew! I knew he existed!
He ominously hissed on my mind that he was there
And would always be there lurking darkly in my backyard
Ambushing my descent from the ladder
To dart his calculated spring.

"Watermelon skins draw snakes," Old Fatima reiterated,
Wobbling her white head wisely.
But deep inside me I knew that if I removed the skin
He would still come back.

So, I said nothing
There in Cleopatra's Alexandria
But buried my hypnotizing secret
Under giant roots of silences
Where I myself
Feared to tread.

Talia and Ada enjoy the beauty of the Caspian Sea in Iran (1977)

BREATHING

I wish to breathe
All my fill
All my depth
Full my lungs
All the time,
Not in gasps
That make me reel
All the more
When breath fades
In arrest.

A faint shallow wisp
Self-taught to hide
In a young
Choking throat
Pricked by words
Piercing looks,
Stealthily gliding
In and out
Half a lung,
Fearful of being heard
By the outside world.

I yearn to breathe
All my fill
In great gulps
Through all my cells
All my branches
All my life...

Spineless Academic

The sleek academic,
what a jelly-fish mess!
His small, round, shallow eyes
blurring out an avalanche
of water-words
over his decaying
piscivorous teeth.

He is incontestably,
a perfect specimen of the
refined image of carp
piscatology is trying to rear
in the civilized, artificial ponds –
sleek, smooth, and almost
spineless.

Take Us To Soweto

Dedicated to the African Black Poets I met in Johannesburg, at the American Embassy (Johannesburg, May, 1977)

Lady from Tel-Aviv, lady from Tel-Aviv,
now that we've read our poems together,
now that we've cried together,
please take us back to Soweto,
with our poems "abalonga goddam"
full of cries of crippled children
full of anger
wrapped in pain –
please take us back
to Soweto.

If I only could, would have taken you
not only to Soweto –
but to where the leaves'
free rustle roams,
where apples and poems grow ripe
before they grow hoarse.

But then, I'm not even
from Tel-Aviv,
I'm only from Haifa –
and have no car
to take you
to the leaves' free rustle,
or to free Soweto.

Ada Aharoni

AFRICA SINGS FREEDOM

Dedicated to President Nelson Mandela
(Written on the occasion of the abolishment of Apartheid)

Inevitable freedom pregnancy
in South Africa's scorched belly.
From Goddess Pomona's throat grows
a triumphant song
fills the air –
Baby Freedom is born!

Africa sings
flying fire-blown icons
exploding into millions of blooming
proteas in flashing rainbow colors
toppling over old Apartheid's grave.
Brave Nelson Mandela waves away the pain
with a grave handshake
and a raised, noble forehead.

The sceptics
thrust their leering grins
deep down their throats,
while Africa joyously sings
the song of glorious
free children carrying
banners full of
protea flowers
filled with promising hopes.

A BICENTENNIAL VISIT TO PLYMOUTH PLANTATION

We walk around modest wooden houses
in the New World
fencing old bearded goats.
'Godly and sober' pilgrims in
colored bonnets and garters
saunter their work (almost)
as in pilgrim past.

A laced minute-man blows an ancient cannon
like an ancient horn. Flash –

Is it possible this great nation
sprouted from this grain of colony
just two short hundred years ago?
New York's skyscrapers,
Boston's universities,
million American hopes
on San Francisco's golden bridge –
it all began here,
in this tiny Mayflower spot
on Plymouth Rock!
The magic of it,
the stupendous feat in a mere Bicentennial
breathes unbound hope –

Now Israel, now global village –
all is possible..

How beautiful upon the mountains are the feet of the
messenger of good tidings that announces peace!
The Bible, Isaiah 52

I am the enemy you killed, my friend.
Wilfred Owen

Ishmael my brother,
Till when shall we fight each other?
Shin Shalom

War is as anachronistic as cannibalism,
slavery and colonialism.
Rosalie Bertell, No Immediate Answer

PART FOUR

YEARNING FOR PEACE

Haim painting his vision of peace,
at the 5th IFLAC Conference in Los Angeles, 1995

I AM NOT IN YOUR WAR ANYMORE.

Surely we cannot paint war green
when even the long Cold War has died.
So let's paint it in all its true
foliage colors, to help its fall.

First, flowing flamboyant crimson blood
on throbbing temples and curly hair,
russet bronze fiery metal cartridges
stuffing the crevices of young hearts,
while golden laser Napalm dragon tongues
gluttonously lick the sizzling eyes and lips
of our children, under giant mushrooms
freshened by mustard and acid rain.

Surely, at the opening of our
promising third millennium
we will soon find the archaic
historical garbage pit
where we can dump
our fearful legacy
forever.

And our grandchildren will ask their fathers,
what were tanks for, Pa? And with eyes
full of wonder, they will read the story of the
glorious imprisonment of the Nuclear Giant
in his hellish dump imprisoned for ever,
and they will cry:
Well done Pa, well done Ma!

Ada Aharoni

I Want to Kill You War

In the fullness of time, war will come to an end,
Not for moral reasons but because of its absurdity
      Evelyne Thomas Hardy

I want to kill you war, forever,
not like a phoenix
that always comes back.

I want to kill you war
and I don't know how
and I don't know why
all the people of the world
don't join hands
to kill you war –
you the greatest murderer
of them all!

The governors of the world
go on feeding your fat belly
with fresh soldiers
and nuclear arms,
with blurring eyes
they only know how to hang
the one or the two
or shoot hundreds of thousands,
but not you –
you the greatest killer
of them all.

After the carnage the priest said
"We are all responsible!"
After the carnage the sheikh said
"We all remain brothers."
After the carnage the rabbi said
"We can stop it if we choose."
The priest, the sheikh and the rabbi
raise up their arms and look up to the sky.

The peace marchers
take hold of the slab of marble
on which is inscribed
"We want to live - not die!"
And carry it away
under the whizzing bullets
like a corpse
still warm
still alive.

MYOPIC SCIENTIST

With green eyes like legend woods
before burning,
waving and sweeping
like sky rockets.

Dear scientist, you were created
for exploring and building,
for love and science and joy
on peaceful green earth,
not to burn, not to destroy our yearnings
with nuclear bombs
and radiation.

Dear scientist, don't let the war merchants
steal your research, your unaware souls,
your creations, your myopic brains.
All our voices radiate in fear,
all our violins sing our impending requiem
brewed in your stupendous high-tech labs.

Dear scientist, let our wings flap freely
in fresh, clean breeze
in the spring and in the fall
before we all fall into the hellish slumber
of a nuclear winter
from which there is no return.

Dear scientist, please
research peace horizons,
say nay to earth wars and star wars,
and any small or big
pitiful, destructive war.

Dear Scientist,
You have already given us so much –
As the Internet I love,
creating friendships and world citizens
in a growing global village.

Now is the time
at the opening
of the second decade
of the third millennium
on our beloved blue planet –
give us the gift of sustainability,
give us the so yearned–for gift
of life in peace
and harmony.

Ada Aharoni

Nuclear Pollution

"After a nuclear winter the living will envy the dead."

When I see a bird
and I say bird
they say bird

When I hear its song
and I say song
they say song

But when I see bombs
and I say bombs –
they say peacemakers

And when I see pollution
and I say radiation
they say – energy

And when I see nuclear pollution
and I say nuclear holocaust
THEY SAY DETERRENCE.

But what kind of deterrence
Can be had
When we are all dead?

HORSES ON ENNISMORE GARDENS

Every day, for three rollicking years
At five o'clock in the morning
They galloped under my curtained windows
Fraying the edges of my dreams
And breaking into the borders of my sleep.

The sound of their brisk trotting
Shot visions of silky browns
Smooth dappled greys
And graceful spotless whites
Flitting through my dimness.

And every day, for three long - short years
I told myself – tomorrow,
Tomorrow I shall surely run to the window
To hail my clippety - cloppety host –
But I never saw the Queen's horses
On Ennismore Gardens.

London 1967

Ada Aharoni

METAL AND VIOLETS IN JERUSALEM

In a time of pomegranates
and yellow balloons,
why are your looks
so bronze-like?
Deep in you
a valve is locked,
and even a warm
yearning clasp
cannot unlock
the metallic clasp.

How can I unpuzzle
your dreams?
I wish I could sow
violets under your pores
until their scent
melted your metal
into mine.

I wish I could place
Jerusalem
in your hand.

ARAB ISRAELI STUDENT ON T.V.

You ponder hard in front of hesitating microphone,
Your eyebrows arch puzzlement over the screen.
Nuances of troubled expression on your
Handsome Semitic face,
Crack and re–crack every query in the air:
"Do I really feel at home here?
And if I do, do they feel I feel at home here,
Am at home here?
Do I feel an Israeli Arab? Or an Arab Israeli?
Or a Palestinian? Or all of these?
Or none of these?"

Suddenly the answer blurts out like a raven in flight
Escaping its dark cage:
"I have no identity!"
The raven flies straight into my eyes with claws and beak,
And I remember my own rootless wound
In Egypt land - and I hurt your dangling hurt,
My Semitic cousin in pain.

The questions stir Nile and Jordan visions
Flowing intense churning –
"And if a Palestinian State is founded
Would you go and live there?
Would you feel better?"
Again the puckered brows lock,
Strained jaw-muscles, glowing sorrowful eyes.

Then gently, like a dove swooping
On its way to peaceful green woods:
"My home is in the Galilee.
But I would feel better if there were
A Palestinian State,
For then my Arab brothers
Would not fight
The land I live in
Any more."

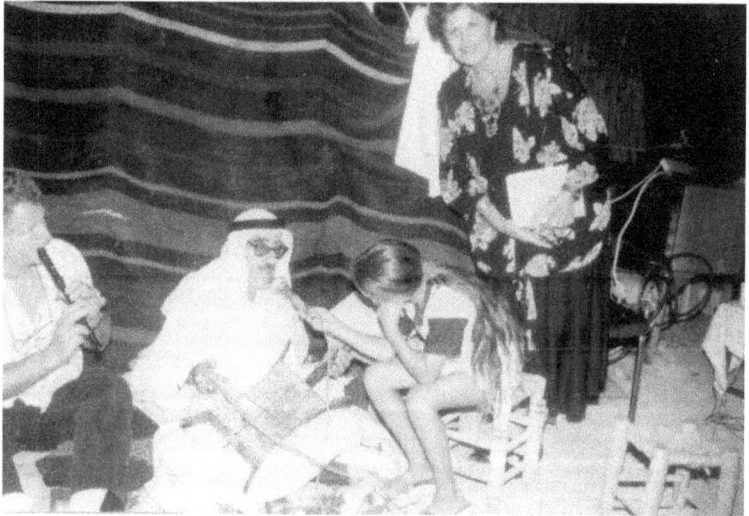

In the Iflac Tent of Peace in Ussfiya on Mount Carmel

RECONCILIATION: THE SULHA POMEGRANATE

ISHMAEL:
Why doesn't Israel explain this more - that you too
And a million other Jews of Arab Lands like you,
Had to spread their wings wide and flee too,
Like me and my Palestinian brothers?

YITZHAK:
Why do you want Israel
To explain this more?
What is it to you? Let the past be past –
Let's open the reconciliation pomegranate

ISHMAEL:
For the past to be past my friend, I have to know.
For me it can be the saving face of Sulha*
The uncovering of the black veil of misunderstanding
On her beautiful and honest face

She proves to me that we Palestinians are not
The only underdogs,
Of the Arab-Israeli conflict –
She shows to me that tragedies,
as in all wars, are on both sides!
It makes it easier for me to
Walk with her on her Sulha path, you see.

YITZHAK:
Good for you Sulha!
Do you mean to say
Ishmael, my brother, that a second tragedy
Can cancel the first one
Or one another?

ISHMAEL:
It is not that two tragedies cancel one another
But it makes it an easier burden to bear
When we know the other has already paid
For the Sulha a long, long time ago...

Wait, don't cut the pomegranate yet.
Now I can identify with you my brother –
As a mutual victim in pain,
And you can identify with me.

YITZHAK:
so now let's open the Sulha Pomegranate
My Palestinian brother, neighbor and friend,
And let's rejoice and flourish together with every
one of its juicy, soothing ruby grains.

Sulha: Reconciliation, in Arabic.

IF A WHITE HORSE FROM JERUSALEM

If a white horse
Straight from Jerusalem,
Strides so valiantly, gracefully
Like yearning
In the early dawn hours
Of my Haifa street,
As if it were the ocean,
As if it were the bright blue sky –
Then all is possible.

Perhaps it has come to take us away –
To peaceful Jerusalem,
It will wink a golden wink
And you will lose your glue
For chains of sand and will fly with me
Perhaps before my hair falls
Before my teeth drop
Before my breath whistles
Before I go.

Perhaps it will lift us
On his white back under his wings
My smile in your palm
Mine in yours –
To Eylat, Cairo and Damascus,
Then back to peaceful Jerusalem.

For if a white horse
From the land of global peace
Strides so valiantly
In my own Horev street –
As if it were the ocean,
As if it were the sky
Then all is possible...

PALM CURVE

Cuddled in the heart of your hand,
soft hand, warm hand,
I do not feel the meaningless drops
of life drizzling,
do not hear its jackal-thunder
nor see its lynx-lightning
in the dark.

And if the world should burst tonight
in a giant mushroom flame,
I would not notice –
snuggled in the nook
of your gentle palm
where I belong,
it seems I may exist
forever.

We are all alike –
gently dozing in the nook
and the noose
of borrowed
nuclear time.

Ada Aharoni

Nuclear Waste on Earth Day

We did not know we were all
dozing on deadly land-mines–
when they dumped their
nuclear waste disposal
in leaking metal cases,
hiding them under the compost pile,
contaminating our groundwater
in our front and back garden.

We did not know,
because they never told us.
They stole stealthily in the dark
and dumped their radiating destruction
in our front and backyard–
without asking our permission.

They knew we would not give it anyway,
so they carefully covered
the deadly nuclear compost pile
with grass clippings
and green leaves, thinking,
those drowsy sunflower people
only turn their heads to the sun,
and will never notice.

But we noticed, and we now
refuse to watch the sunshine
when nuclear fire is burning
under our roots.

KILLING ME SOFTLY

"If we are honest with ourselves we have to admit that unless we
rid ourselves of our nuclear arsenals a holocaust not only might
occur but will occur if not today, then tomorrow ...
We have come to live on borrowed time."
    Jonathan Schell, The Fate of the Earth

We wise grown-ups often advise our children
"Stop fighting, you will hurt each other,"
then calmly proceed to annihilate one another.
We breed black widows with red eyes in our labs.

War is eternal, you say.
Listen, my brother,
War's second cousin, "dueling,"
was once sung immortal,
the peak of honor -
yet it has been banished and is no more.

Slavery was also deemed eternal.
So why do you go on killing us
with your guns and scuds?
Does a lioness devour her cubs?
Does a gardener destroy his buds?

The absurd "deterrence" mantra
has also to go
for now we know,
in a nuclear war
there are no winners
there are only dead bodies
on all sides.

Let's wake up
before we breed more black widows
with red eyes in our labs.

WHAT IS PEACE FOR ME?

Peace for me is a flowing golden river,
students fresh from school,
with minds
full of pockets of hope

Not after they witnessed
their friends' brains
blown white-veined
on white sands, still thinking.

Peace for me
is to visit
Kadreya in Egypt, and
my house in Midan Ismaileya, in Cairo
now Tahrir – the Square of Freedom –
where I was born, and evicted.

To place again my open palm
on the Sphinx's paw,
and check if now I'm as tall
as a Pyramid stone.

Peace for me
is all this, my friend,
and so much more –
when I look at you our golden children
and feel the next war
pinching the center of my heart.

Peace Poet Wilfred Owen

WILFRED OWEN: WE ARE STILL DEAF
BUT NOT DUMB ANYMORE

Dear Wilfred Owen*
You sang
You warned
You died
And we are still deaf.

Our sons' teeth
Are still for laughing
Round an apple,
Yet now we tie
Not only bayonet-blades to them
But also super Super Sams.

Their trembling limbs
Are not only knife-skewed nowadays
But Napalm-roasted beyond recognition –
We have come a long way
In the killing game.

Wilfred Owen, you shouted:
The absurdity of war
The pity of war!
And we are still deaf
For those who still die in battle as cattle.

Yet the day will soon come
Before time falls from the clock,
When war will become
A demoded anachronism.

Wilfred Owen, you sang, you warned,
You cried, you died,
And yet our leaders are still deaf, so deaf,
Stupidly, stupidly deaf.

You have shown us what a poet can do
To open the manacled doors
Of consciousness wide
When you spoke to me so deeply
Through your powerful poems
Already at the age of fifteen.

And I promise you, dear Wilfred Owen,
We will not be deaf nor dumb anymore –
We at IFLAC* will continue your road
Under your white flag, until
We overcome the Satanic concept and
Diabolic practice of war.

* *Wilfred Owen – A famous British Peace Poet who died in the trenches in the First World War. Ada Aharoni studied his poems at school in Egypt, and since then they deeply influenced her view of life, of war and of peace, and in the founding of IFLAC.*

* *IFLAC: The International Forum for the Literature and Culture of Peace, founded by Ada Aharoni in 1999.*
www.iflac.wordpress.com

TO AN EGYPTIAN SOLDIER

Dedicated to the Egyptian Pilot who appeared on Israeli television
during the Yom Kippur War in October 1973

I saw you on television last night
bewildered in our land,
your eyes were dim
and you mumbled under your shield:
"I want to go back to my young wife
and four-year-old son."

And I wanted to tell you
Egyptian soldier,
I know that this time you did not run away
because they told you
this land is yours
clutch it back with firm hand.
Yet tonight, under Israeli skies
you ask yourself:
"Why am I here
and not with my young wife and child?"

You see, Egyptian soldier,
you will always have your Nile
and your bed to turn to,
but if we lose there's only the sea.

Ada Aharoni

I hope you go back to your wife
and four-year-old son soon,
and our fathers come back to theirs,
this time, after a quarter of a century of strife,
with the long longed–for
trophy of peace
for all.

UNICORN IN MANHATTAN'S CLOISTERS

To my friend Tahita, and to the memory of dear Ralph,
who both introduced me to the magnificent unicorn.

In the Metropolitan Museum,
I watch you in gobelin tapestry
from the 15th century –
white unicorn in the arms of forests
trailed and ambushed in all green places
by well-known piercing, hunting eyes
flashing odious machinations
from your century to mine –
witness of Bergen-Belsen's
human-skin lampshades.

I shudder under your limpid betrayed eye
tear-dewing my flesh.
The sharp long-nosed lances
piercing red your snowy flanks –
burrow my own bones,
as you desperately raise your front legs
and our mutual uni-corn
to freedom from the piranha.
I drown in the eely tentacles
of your blood-stained wound.

I know what it is
to be
a hunted, betrayed
unicorn.

New York, May 1976

Ada Aharoni

THE SAPLING OF PEACE

On the occasion of the Geneva Convention,
17 December 1973

The mothers bore children,
The children had to go to war.
In October, children ceased to be;
End of October, the fire ceased.

The distraught mothers and fathers
And what was left of their children,
Could do naught in their scorching sorrow
But plant, a frail sapling
In the desert sand
Under the burnt skeleton of tanks
Fringed with human limbs
No shade or crutch could help.

The sapling was carried to Geneva
By sure hands,
Was watered by the blue lake,
By the Bible and the Koran,
And by the wise Tagore
Who sang of love.

Despite its desert origins:
The years of passion and fire
Inflaming the thorns of anger and despair,
The sapling sprouted tiny green leaves
With amazing patterns
Of kaleidoscopic dewdrops
Of hope of peace.

Ada Aharoni

This Cursed War

*Inspired by an Israeli Soldier's Yom Kippur War Diary,
found in the Golan Heights, October 1973.*

The night creeps long, funeral throng
Memories rush and flood blood.
Blossoming list of dead thumps red.
Every name pins mind with whizzing missiles,
   Cursed, cursed war!

In jeep on Golan Heights, loneliest I have ever been,
I watch skeletons of tanks, crowned with names of friends,
Sorrowful, sinister row, black graves,
Fresh bodies - old smell,
   Cursed, cursed war!

It doesn't look at all like wars in films this war,
Here we do not get a chance to shoot, or wave a flag,
Shrieking shells, hyena lightning pour on us,
And we run backwards or forwards or to the side,
And some are saved and some are not,
Not all, not always; but always cursing
   This cursed, cursed war!

In an English centurion holding Belgian guns,
We watch two American-made airplanes
Shot down by Russian-made missiles.
I cannot hate the Syrian on the other side
Who holds a French gun and shoots Soviet Sams;
For we are toy soldiers of astute shopkeepers
Who want to sell - selling us, in this
       Cursed, cursed war!

God, let it stop, let it end,
Let the nightmare end!
Cursing is the only shelter
I can creep into,
As into a mother's womb,
Not to crumble before thoughts in the dark.
Cursed are those who force me to be here
Cursed be this cursed, cursed war!

Ada Aharoni

REMEMBER ME EVERY TIME THE MOON RISES ABOVE THE SPHINX

Inspired by an Egyptian soldier's diary found in the Sinai,
after the Yom Kippur War (October 1973)

Dear Leila, to you my love
I breathe my last letter.
I love you in all the ways love means,
Remember me every time the sun sets over the
Pyramids and the moon rises over the Sphinx

Today marks the ninth year
Of my enrolling at the cursed military college.
If I knew then to what bitter thorns it would lead me –
The college would have never seen my face.
I loathe the hours a man goes through
While waiting for death.

Remember me every time the sun sets over the Pyramids
and the moon rises over the Sphinx

I really believed what we were told,
That we Egyptians, would never begin a war –
But we have been ordered to cross the Suez Canal,
and my blood, my bones know
I just have a few more hours to live.

I will fight and die for Allah and Egypt –
When what I want is to live
For you, my Leila,
Loving you all my life,
My Leila, my love,
My life.

Ada Aharoni

FOR THOSE WHO DIE AS CATTLE

"What passing-bells for those who die as cattle?
Only the monstrous anger of the guns...."
Wilfred Owen

They met at right angles
of a white marble tomb,
then off again on spirals
of darkness and sorrow,
he with his deft trigger fingers
on guns,
she with her green fingers
on chrysanthemums.

I'm moved you remembered him –
she whispered,
you remembered the passing bells
for my son who died in battle.

How could I forget
the monstrous anger
of the guns that killed
my brave soldier, your son.

I miss him so, she wept,
why should he give his life
when he had not yet
started to live?
Oh God, why?

Her painful words and tears
like sharp spears
in his ears
sprinkled on her son's tomb
flew with the swift wind,
and were echoed
far and wide.

Ada Aharoni

No Talking

The politicians decided –
No talking with the enemy
Beat them because they attack us
Shed their blood and that of their leaders
But most of all –

NO TALKING!

In the meantime, in Israel
And in the heart of Gaza
Blood flows and legs are blown away
And little eight-year-old Twito from Sderot
And eight-year-old Mohamed from Gaza
Will not play football anymore
But –

NO TALKING!

How can we convince violent leaders
To talk and not to shoot?
I watch from the side
At the tragic hen and egg situation
And weep together with all the
Innocent people from both sides,
But still, first and foremost –

NO TALKING!

SOUNDS OF PEACE

Ships hoot from Haifa port,
sounds of peace leap up to me
from every jewel in Mount Carmel's crown,
while the azure Mediterranean
winks at me
reassuringly
below the bright blue horizon.

The eventful year 2012 leans over me and
enlaces my arm, with
President Shimon Peres' Award*
bringing joy to my heart
that our peace sounds have been heard.

Now it is towards 2013 I turn
and give it a hopeful long yearned–for
welcoming peace kiss.

* On September 4, 2012, Ada Aharoni was awarded the President
Shimon Peres Award, for the spreading of the Culture of Peace.

Talia my rare "Rare Flower"

PART FIVE

TALI MY RARE FLOWER

Talia Winkler, my brave and wonderful daughter, passed away at the age of 55, on July 8, 2011, after a courageous struggle against cancer, for thirteen eventful years, in which she so bravely continued enjoying life, creating, dancing and singing.

A LYRICAL MEMORY

Under the stars and the fragrant trees
In Tali's and Avi's home in Nofit in the Galilee,
Tali's friends sang with us the songs she loved.
With soft voices we tread on steps of sorrow
And up the ladder to the heights of love
Tali offered us with all her heart.

The full colors of our voices
In music and in words softly sang you Tali,
In a symphonic lyrical memory
Of our fairy goddess who with her
Magic wand and wondrous smile
Mysteriously knew how to solve all.

We sang the peace songs you loved Tali
And the distance between the songs and the skies
Became a bunch of promising flowers
Shedding away with their fragrance
The borders between you and the music –
And suddenly you were among us Tali,
Singing your beautiful life song.

Tali My Beautiful Rare Flower

What a terrible lack of justice! What pain!
We educated you for love, honesty and giving,
To honor life, peace, and humankind –
And this is how you grew;
This is how you lived,
An angel on earth,
A beautiful, rare flower, plucked before her time!
What a terrible lack of justice! What pain!

You were wise, with a heart of gold,
Lovely and so gifted!
Despite your painful suffering due to your cruel cancer,
You never complained, you never cried,
Went on caring for your family with warmth and devotion,
To dance and sing, to direct your excellent "Nofit Choir",
And to lecture on the boons of Social Work, and the
"Importance of the Development of Memory"
At the exemplary "Dorot" college,
Which you founded in the Galilee.

Your wonderful husband and three children
And even tiny, sweet Lotem, your first granddaughter,
Helped you to bear the pain.
We all stood by you holding your gentle, noble hand
Till the bitter end.
What a terrible lack of justice! What pain!

Even then, you courageously smiled
Your enchanting, hopeful smile,
And this is how we will always remember you
Tali, My Beautiful Rare Flower,
Rest in Peace.

Your loving mother
Ada

Tiny Tali smiling on her mother's lap

Ada Aharoni

A Birthday of Love

Talia is six years old
She is in the first class
And she loves all the children.
To her birthday party she invites
The whole class.

You are also inviting unruly Yossi?
Her friends asked in dismay,
Have you forgotten he spoiled
Ella's birthday and threw chocolate
Cake at all the children!

I have already invited Yossi
And at my birthday party
He will not throw chocolate cakes
But sunflower petals,
Talia laughed and said

Well-combed Yossi arrived
Wearing a bright white new shirt
In one hand he carried
A gift pen and in the other
Jasmine flowers for smiling Talia

Talia hugged and kissed Yossi,
She invited him to sit next to her
And to be the first to play
The Flower Game
With the sunflower petals she prepared

Yossi threw his sunflower petal
High up and it fell on Talia's shining curls
Yossi kissed her joyfully
And at that moment
Yossi was born again!

Talia, said the teacher Nehama,
Since your Birthday of Love
Yossi has changed so much
Not only in his behavior
But even in his lessons

Talia you are a real angel
That performs miracles!

Ada Aharoni

TALIA SAVES THE CAT

When Talia was seven years old
On her return from school
She saw a group of children
Standing silent and afraid.
In the middle stood eleven year-old Ian
With a sharp knife in his hand!
He was preparing to cut the tail
Of a poor black cat he had tied to a pole.
The cat shrieked at the top of its lungs help, help
In miaou language, but nobody moved.

Brave little Talia stood in front of
Big, cruel Ian and cried out to him:
You think you are stronger than the cat
But my father is stronger than you
And what you do to the cat
He will do to you!

Ian's mouth opened in surprise,
His big knife dropped to the ground
And he ran away to his home.
The children helped Talia to untie the cat
It threw a grateful look at Talia and ran away.
Good for you Talia, said the children
And with large smiles
They patted her on her back.

Talia smiled in relief when she
Related the story to her parents.
Her mother asked: but weren't you afraid
Of mad Ian?
Yes I was very afraid said Talia
Afraid for the poor cat!

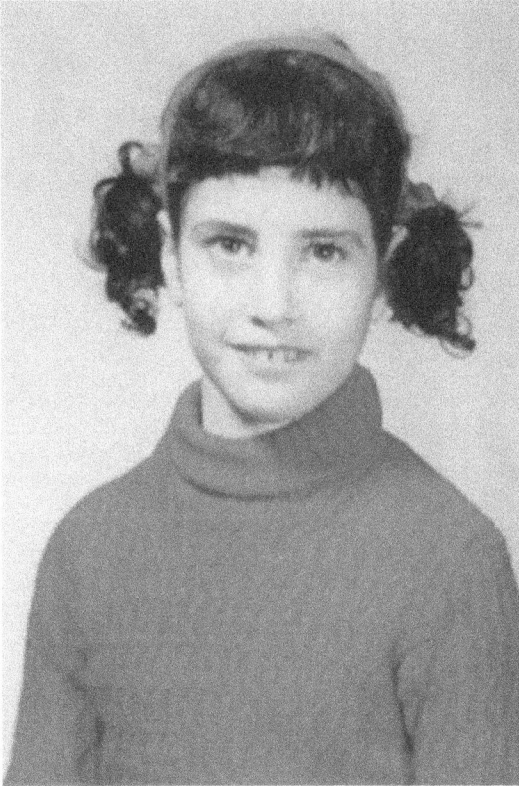

Tali at seven, after she saved the cat

Tali on bycicle in Iran

Haim and Ada with Talia and Avi at their Wedding

I wrote the next poem when we thought Talia was cured, after she came back radiant from the cancer clinic in Denmark, in June 2009. But the cancer came back two years later and infiltrated her bones. Now she rests in peace, and dances, sings and twinkles in our hearts and with the stars forever ...

A COURAGEOUS DAUGHTER CALLED TALI

She had twinkling honey-green eyes
and velvety black curls –
she laughed in the wind
and sang and danced under the trees with the stars
Tali, Tali, Tali, Tali

"You have breast-cancer that has spread"
the doctors curtly said –
"Chimio-Therapy all the rest of your three months' life!"
She stopped laughing in the wind
and stopped singing and dancing with the stars
Tali, Tali, Tali, Tali

"I won't let you poison me anymore!"
she firmly said and fled
from the Chimio-Therapy trap –
to grass-juice, green vegetables and fruit
Tali, Tali, Tali, Tali
She won, she triumphed!
She laughs again in the wind
she dances again with the stars –
my lovely, courageous daugther
Tali, Tali, Tali, Tali

The Bat–Mitzva of Nitzan, Tali's daughter (12 years old).

Ada Aharoni

Departure

You lay on the couch as a last rose of summer
Tali my rare flower
"This time too you will overcome, you'll see,
As you succeeded every time" I said,
And I wanted to hug you to my heart my daughter
And to give you my life for yours.

"This time it is harder than ever, ma,"
You said with a serious smile
Of a last rose of summer.
"More difficult than the operation?"
"Yes, more difficult than the operation"
You murmured, as if you had solved at last
The mystery of life.

A sharp knife delved into me
And I wanted so to hug you to my heart my daughter
And to give you my life for yours,
Tali my rare flower.
You gave me your lovely, delicate hand and
Whispered, thank you for all ma,
Shalom Ima.

I kissed the frail, beloved hand
And tried to plant violets of strength into it.
It was my last kiss
The kiss of departure
The next day you were gone,
Tali, my rare, rare flower!

Your loving mother who misses you so much!

Tali with Itai and Ori in Wisconsin

Tali preparing for climbing

STOP THE TEARS

There is nothing in the world harder
Than to lose a daughter!
Enough of drowning in the sea of tears
Sorrow is a never ending trap
That swallows all my entity, all my hours, all my plans,
Everything seems to me to be shallow, tasteless,
Lacking any horizon, without any goal
Without Tali.

However, this is not what Tali expected of me,
"Go on with your struggle for peace ma,"
She whispered, "For both
Of us, when I am not here."

I have to follow her example
To honor her memory, her optimistic life
Full of harmony, peace and hope,
To follow her spirit for the creation of a better society,
A better Middle East, a better world –
Without violence, destruction, terror and famine,
A new world at peace with itself and far beyond war.

Stop the tears, the work of peace
Is tremendous and Tali expects me to continue
For both of us, and indeed we will all continue
To build your loving peace path Tali, through IFLAC –
In your spirit, with your devotion and with
Your wise angelic smile.

Tali and granddaughter Lotem

Tali and daughter Nitzan

Ada Aharoni

Your Life Song Tali Will Go On Forever

You Tali, were an angel on earth
You spread your wings and your smiles to all,
You sang a symphony of courageous
Hope, love and peace –
My immortal daughter Tali.

I promise you Tali, your life song –
The creation of a family of love,
Your wonderful "Dorot" club
That gave joy and knowledge to all
And the directing of the excellent "Nofit" choir,
All your creations will go on for generations
Your symphony will not be forgotten
We will continue to sing it with all our souls –
My immortal daughter Tali.

We will continue the peace train voyage
Of your life Tali,
To create, to sing, to love, to speak peace,
And like you, with kindness, grace and humility,
To respect each other, to embrace life
And all people, no matter what faith they are –
People from all the nations of our global village.

I promise you Tali
We will continue the paving of your road,
We will promote with your smile and your embrace
The Jewish motto you cherished –
"Tikkun Olam" – the repairing of our world,
The creation of a beautiful global village
Beyond war and violence –
In your memory dear Tali
My immortal daughter.

Tali Winkler, Director of Dorot

Tali, Avi, and the three children, at Itai's wedding, Tali's eldest son standing on the left.

PART SIX

IN MEMORY OF HAIM

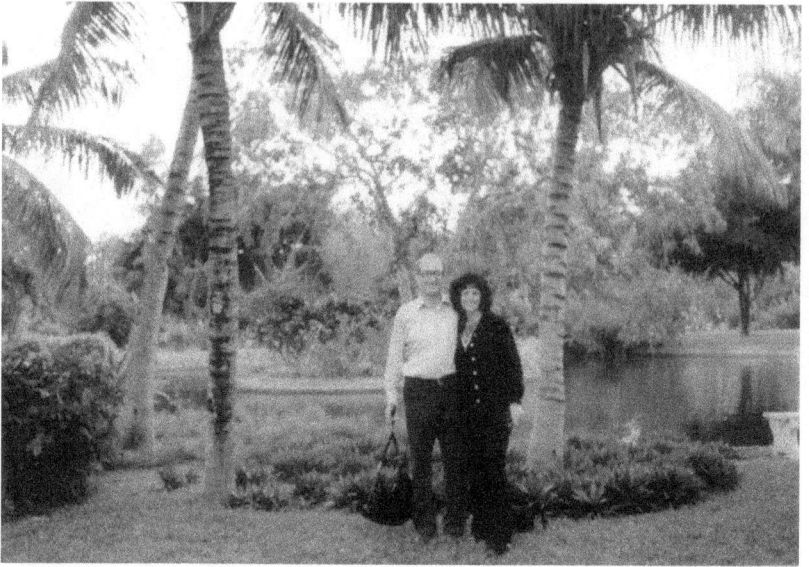

*Haim and Ada during a wonderful holiday in the Bahamas (1981)
to celebrate thirty years of marriage*

Haim feeding a Kangaroo in Australia

Ada Aharoni

To Haim – To Life

Since you passed away, dear Haim,
My loving companion
For three quarters of my life
Your absence is at my side
Like a flowing river
That lost its silvery ripples
Lost its luster in the mist

I miss you so, my wise "Richelieu"
With your combination of ripples of
Gentleness, intelligence and firmness.
Your smile will not enter my room anymore
But it is in my heart forever like
A constant flowing river
Of ripe words clinging to my cells

You whispered on your deathbed:
"Now you will have to work doubly hard
On promoting the culture of peace
As I will not be here to help you…"
But you are here and helping me, my friend,
Your warm voice flows in me constantly –
You are still so much with me
My Haim – My Life.

*My dear departed husband Haim passed away on July 6, 2006.
Haim in Hebrew means "Life".

Haim and Ada near the statue of "The Scientist."
Haim was a Professor of Chemical Engineering
at the Technion in Haifa.

Ada Aharoni

WE ALL LEARNED FROM YOU

Haim my cherished love,
during all your fruitful existence
we all learned from you,
from your love, your strength, and determination
to serve humanity, science, and peace,
we enjoyed your lucidity
your maverick brightness,
your infinite modesty.

You lived in full harmony with yourself
and with all who surrounded you,
you knew you were loved and admired
and you loved us all in return
with armfuls of calm golden sunbeams
in your eager, bright eyes
full of twinkling stars
of love and knowledge.

Hundreds of loving friends
came to pay their condolences and they too all
said how much they learned from you
each one in his own way, admired you,
and I expected every moment for the door to open
and for you to come in to welcome all your friends –
I waited and waited –
but you did not come.

*Haim, Ada, Ariel, Tali, and Ada's brother Claude,
feeding the birds in Trafalgar Square, London (1967).*

Ada Aharoni

Our Beautiful New Home

I was a pale
ivory tower, surrounded
by white marble slabs
until you came
into my house and it became our home

You deftly climbed my hidden stairs
gently pushed open my secret windows,
alighting upon vaulted mosaic
my curves smoothly responded to
your precise angles

I offered you my heart as fireplace
my hands as gloves
to keep you warm,
my ears as vessels
for your words

Laying the pearls of your life
on my hearth
you lit my fireplace
filled me with warmth,
lonely tower became cozy new home

I am glad you came to inhabit me
before our summer was spent,
before we both tumbled down
in the mighty tornado
of the infinite unknown

Though you have passed away my love
You still inhabit me
In our beautiful new home
On the top of the world
With the moon and the stars
And the dazzling flying comets.

Haim and Ada in Greece

Ada Aharoni

WHAT IS HAPPINESS?

When you were here dear Haim,
One bright golden day I asked you
"What Is Happiness"?
You promptly responded
With a bright twinkle in your eye
"Happiness is being married to your best friend"
I laughed and hugged you my best friend.

Now that you have passed away my love
And we will not talk and laugh together anymore
I miss your kisses and warm hugs
I miss your caressing, gentle calm
With which you appeased all storms,
I admire your spirit that fights my sorrow
That sings "Be Happy" in spite of all –
For this is my legacy.

Haim and Ada in a rain forest in Queensland, Australia

COFFEE FOR TWO

Dedicated to the memory of my dear Haim,
written on the sixth anniversary of his departure, July 7, 2012

Coffee for two
is life shared
in harmony, in safety
joy, peace
and love

Coffee for two
is sharing each other's
hopes, thoughts, tribulations
and fears of manipulations
by crafty war-mongers

Coffee for two
assures me your memory will always
be hugging me safely my love
always be a full cup
of love, of hope, of life

Even now
when you are not
here anymore, the warm aroma
of Coffee for two
warms my heart.

Haim and Ada on the Great Wall of China

PART SEVEN

LEBANON POEMS

Inspired from Letters of Israeli Soldiers

written while serving in Lebanon

I'M NOT RETURNING HOME

I'm so sorry, my love,
I'm not returning home
for I can't return
home.

I love you so,
want to be with you so,
but somewhere there –
among Lebanon's majestic cedars
so far from you my love –
I was hit by a murderous bullet
in the center of
the fallow of my heart
where I first fell for you
forever.

I so want to be with you my love,
so want to hug you
my love, my life –
but cannot return home.
They have uselessly, pitifully,
spilled my young life, my blood,
under Lebanon's blue sky,
and now I feel I will not,
just cannot
return home.

Ada Aharoni

THE HELL WITH WAR

They announced a cease-fire
But they continued to bomb us
And we continued to bomb
Their Beyrut Airport
And the streets and the houses,
What is it with them?
And what is it with us?

I loathe killing, I hate destroying,
Horrible, pitiful war!
Why should we allow them
To force us to be here?
And what hence?
And when will it end?
The Hell with War!

Mr. Prime Minister, When Will The Nightmare End?

Mr. Prime Minister,
when will the nightmare end?
What absolute misery –
I want to go home!
Instead of home's warmth,
anguished cold in my frozen bones
while watching the dreadful shock of a man
who has just discovered his dead wife's body
under his wrecked home

We came back from the nightmare
with horror in our hearts
and imploring in our eyes –
Mr. Prime Minister, we were born
for creation, for joy and life –
not for destruction!
Please, Mr. Prime Minister,
end this nightmare that really kills –
and not only in our nightmares.

Ada Aharoni

SECURITY IS A SIAMESE TWIN

For our security, our safety –
we will break their teeth,
for our security, our safety,
we will throw tons of bombs
on their heads and on their safety,
on their orchards
and on their veins and on their vines,
on their houses and on their pride –
all this only for our security.

But where is our security, our safety?
And what about their security, their safety?
In truth, our security and their security
Are Siamese Twins –
in reality, you can't hit one
without the other.

THE LIE THAT EXPLODED

That night the big lie exploded
like a huge volcano
in my heart and in my mind
shattering all my limbs
and my former values.

That huge volcanic lie
that violence can stop conflicts
exploded in the very depth
of my mind and heart
together with the shrieking bombs.

And on that illuminating
explosive night –
my very dreams exploded
with that tremendous
duping lie.

Ada Aharoni

WHEN WE WILL GO BACK HOME

When we will go back home
They will not trick us anymore,
When we will return home
We will show them
What peace is.

When we will go back home
We will hug our joyful wives and children,
And we will try to forget the sadness
In the eyes of their wives and children,
We will try, we will try very hard –
But I know we will never
Forget.

BACH IN BEYRUT

A moment of harmony in Beyrut –
We suddenly heard from one of the houses
Bach music beautifully played –
The whole company stopped
To hear the music.

The pianist played beautifully
and the whole company
Listened to the exquisite harmony.
The bombs did not succeed to stop us –
But a sixteen year old girl
Playing Bach music
Stopped us!

Ada Aharoni

Amputated Hand

A young boy runs to me
and asks for a sweet,
he spreads his amputated arm
without a hand –

"Who did that to you?"
I ask aghast,
"Entum!" – "You!"
he answers timidly –
his apologetic bashfulness
strangles
my shocked
shame.

FEAR FROM A MOSQUITO

We are forced to be policemen
of a Lebanese population that hates us –
Moslems, Christians and Druze,
with thorny conflicts among them –
yet they all agree on one thing –
they all hate us!

We have entered a muddy morass
in which we are drowning –
Oh God! What a mess!
And in the end
we only found a mosquito –
but its bite kills,
and we shouldn't be here!
Oh God! What a mess,
Four Peace Mothers, please save us!

Ada Aharoni

To A Captain in the Sinai Desert

I howled before the dawn appeared,
the restless bed
creaked in fear
beneath my banging shoulder,
while the pit in my throat
grew and grew
like a yawning crater.

Since you were clutched away
to the Judgment Day War –
the sun is black sand.
Bombs in black sackcloth
float under my breath
exploding it,
making a choking icicle
of me.

Before the night dies again
on my lips,
flash a sign from the desert
my love,
make a sign of life –
so that I can live –
ending howls in sounds
of peace.

A Mother's Letter

You will not build a nest
dear Gili,
every night you return to me,
and your silent cries
silence my heart,
"Mother, mother, help me!"
And I cannot

I can only caress the rugged stone
over your bones,
as I used to caress your soft curls
before sleeping ...

Ada Aharoni

THE FOUR MOTHERS

Leave Lebanon In Peace

(Can be sung to the music of "Let My People Go!")

When soldier sons were in Lebanon Land,
Let the soldiers go!
They suffered so much they could not stand,
Let the Soldiers go!
Go up Four Peace Mothers,
Liberate your soldier sons,
Biblical Revka, Sarah, Leah, Rachel –
Let our sons go!

The soldiers under the cedar trees
Heard the four mothers in joy –
Leave Lebanon, Leave Lebanon,
Leave Lebanon in Peace,
They sang and laughed in joy –

Go home soldiers,
Go home to Israel Land
And leave, and leave
Leave Lebanon in Peace!

Thoughtful, dreamy and optimistic Talia

PART EIGHT

ISRAELI POETS

Translated from Hebrew

by Ada Aharoni

Poet Shin Shalom with Ada, joyful at the publishing of the first GALIM Peace Literature and Culture Magazine (1985)

Three Poems by Shin Shalom

The late Shin Shalom, one of the greatest Israeli poets, was born in Poland in 1904, and in 1922 he settled in Palestine. He became President of the Israeli Writers' Association, and he won wide acclaim and numerous prizes in Israel and abroad. His poems were translated from Hebrew to English by Ada Aharoni, and were published in two books (POEMS: Eked, Tel Aviv, 1981;and NEW POEMS, 1985, available on amazon.com).

Ishmael, Ishmael

Ishmael my brother,
How long shall we fight each other?

My brother from times bygone,
My brother, Hagar's son,
My brother the wandering one,
One angel was sent to us both,
One angel watched over our growth,
You in the wilderness dying of thirst,
I a sacrifice on the altar, Sara's first.

Ishmael my brother hear my plea –
It was the angel who tied you to me,
The caravan of life progresses
Why steal our children's breath
And bring us all to death?
Why should we blind each other's eyes?
Let us be brothers – brother arise!

Ishmael, Ishmael,
How long shall we fight each other?
The hatred has narrowed our minds,
Let's not forget our common father Av-ram,
Let's throw away conflict and mistrust
Let's again be brothers
And live in peace
Side by side.

Shin Shalom
Translated from Hebrew by Ada Aharoni

Triple Thread

To believe in what?
In the seed.

To do what?
To be.

Why do I live?
To give.

* Life is indeed a triple thread...
The Bible – Ecclesiastes

Shin Shalom
Translated from Hebrew by Ada Aharoni

SERAPH

I was sent to raise
To raise the world,
The whole earth to raise

I could not find where
The base and basis were
The base of the world to raise

It broke and fell
And floated in space,
In space where no raising can be

And I after it
Aflame and burning
Burning to raise the world.

Shin Shalom
Translated from Hebrew by Ada Aharoni

THREE POEMS BY AMIR GILBOA

*The late Amir Gilboa, born in the Ukraine in 1917,
came to Palestine in 1937 and became one of Israel's
most important peace poets.*

In Darkness

If they show me a stone
And I say stone, they say stone.

If they show me wood
And I say wood, they say wood.

But if they show me blood
And I say blood, they say paint.

IF THEY SHOW ME BLOOD
AND I SAY BLOOD!
THEY SAY PAINT.

Amir Gilboa
Translated from Hebrew by Ada Aharoni

I Opened the Door

I opened my door
and many, many crowded to come in.
I therefore pushed back
the walls of my room
to welcome all my guests.
And my room
became the home
of my friends
and my room became the world.

Amir Gilboa
Translated from Hebrew by Ada Aharoni

Who Did Everything On Time?

Who did everything on time?
Neither did I.
Not even after time.
And all the present time melted
In flashes of liquid moments.

With me
Even the highest mountains
liquefy.

Amir Gilboa
Translated from Hebrew by Ada Aharoni

THREE POEMS BY YEHUDA AMICHAI

The late Yehuda Amichai (1924 – 2000) was a universally re-
nowned peace poet, and his books were translated into numerous
languages. Many of his poems were put to music,
and he received several prestigious awards and prizes.

On Yom Kippur

On Yom Kippur in the year Tashkah,
I wore dark festive clothes
and ambled to the old quarter
in Jerusalem.
I stood a long time
before an Arab's nook-shop
not far from the Gate of Shechem,
a shop of buttons and zippers and rolls of thread
of all colors, and tic-tacs and buckles.

Suddenly, a bright light shone forth
with many colors
like an open tabernacle

And I told him in my heart that my father too
had a shop like his of threads and buttons,
I explained to him in my heart
about all the sorrowful decades of years
and the sad events and causes
that I am now here
and my father's shop is burnt there
and he is buried here.

When I finished it was closing time,
he too pulled the blind and locked the gate.
And I went back home with all those
who went to pray.

Yehuda Amichai
Translated from Hebrew by Ada Aharoni

THE BUS STATION

The bus that will take me home
Will take you away from me.
We shall never meet.

The tin plate
With the number
Will ring in the wind
Like my heart.

Yehuda Amichai
Translated from Hebrew by Ada Aharoni

Battlefield Rain

It rains on my friends' faces
On my living friends'
Blanket-covered heads
And on my dead friends'
Uncovered faces.

Yehuda Amichai
Translated from Hebrew by Ada Aharoni

The following two poets, the late Zelda, and the late Leah Goldberg, were two of the greatest women poets in Modern Israeli Literature.

LONELY DRUM

They loved me very much
Until I was brought to the gallows,
They loved me very much,
But I was brought to the gallows.
They did not say if good or bad
The day I was taken to the gallows,
And so happened what happened
And I was brought to the gallows.

Sole drum, sole drum
Raps in the town,
Lonely drum, lonely drum
To the end of town,
Lonely drum, lonely drum
Rolls in the road,
Today the dead will be buried
And nobody cries.

I was brought to the gallows
The forests were silent,
I was brought to the gallows
The rivers were silent.
I was brought to the gallows
All the streets were silent
I was brought to the gallows
None came out of the houses.

Sole drum, sole drum
Clamors in the town,
Lonely drum, lonely drum
To the end of town,
Lonely drum, lonely drum
Rolls in the roads
Today the dead will be buried
And there is no shroud.

Leah Goldberg
Translated from Hebrew by Ada Aharoni

Every Rose

Every rose is an island
Of promised peace.
In the eternal peace
In every rose
There dwells
A bird of sapphire
Whose name is 'Ve Kitetu' –
Whose name is – peace,
When they magically transformed
Their swords into plowshares

The light of the rose
Seems so near,
So near its fragrance,
So near is the silence
Of its leaves,
So near
The island of peace –
Take a boat
And cross the sea
Of fire.

Zelda
Translated from Hebrew by Ada Aharoni

Erez Biton

Erez biton was the Head of the Israeli Writers Association.
He was born in Algiers and now lives in Israel.
He was blinded by a land mine
when he was playing in a field at the age of 12.

Fallen Soldier in the Middle East

A father (Jewish or Arab) mourning
the death of his son

And we, what are we?
Just wandering souls
Like foundations of crumbling houses

And I wished that you would be
An olive tree
That blossoms and promises fruit
That bears within it a riddle
Of ripe old age.
And I wished that you would be
A palm tree
Rooted by the banks of flowing rivers

And I know they will all come now
To present their condolences...
But all I wish for is that you be
That you be
Here

Erez Bitton
Translated from Hebrew by Ada Aharoni

Judith Zilbershtein

Judith Zilbershtein is a poet and artist, who lives in Haifa. She was a member of the Board of Directors of IFLAC: PAVE PEACE in Israel , and editor of GALIM Peace Literature Magazine Nos. 8, 9, 10, together with Editor in chief Ada Aharoni.

Ada with artist and poet Judith Zilbershtein joyfully participating in IFLAC celebration for the publication of GALIM 9

COME LET US MEET

Come let us meet
At the crossroad
Like isotherms, different and common
In a meteorological peace map

Come let us meet
At the crossroad
Like isotopes
Not otherwise –
Chemical elements
Different and similar

Come let us meet, like brothers and sisters
All sons and daughters of our Father Abraham,
Let us reject hatred and hot-headedness,
Let's not lose the golden hour
And go on playing
Neptune and Pluto games
Of never meeting

Let us meet at the crossroad
On the silver lining in the horizon
And turn it into a wonderful
Golden path to peace.

Judith Zilbershtein
Translated from Hebrew by Ada Aharoni

And from India

Rabindranath Tagore

Late National Hindu Poet of India

Stream of Life

The same stream of life
that runs through my veins day and night
runs through the world
and dances in rhythmic measure.
It is the same life
that shoots in joy through the dust of the earth
in numberless blades of grass
and breaks into tumultuous waves
of leaves and flowers.
It is the same life
that is rocked in the ocean-cradle of birth and death,
in ebb and flow.

I feel my limbs are made glorious
by the touch of this world of life.
And my pride is from the life-throb of ages
dancing in my blood at this moment.

PART NINE

POEMS BY ADA AHARONI TRANSLATED INTO VARIOUS LANGUAGES

THREE POEMS IN FRENCH

French is Ada Aharoni's mother tongue, she writes in three languages: English, French and Hebrew.

Je consacre les deux suivants poèmes à la mémoire de mon cher père – Nessim Yadid (Diday), du Caire et de Paris.

Ada Aharoni

LE SECOND EXODE

Aujourd'hui j'apporte à nouveau
Mon vaisseau
De grain
A ton port père,
En humant l'odeur de blé
Que tu aimais –
Moi dans le Silo Dagon à Haifa,
Toi là-bas, si loin, si près.

Joseph en Egypte,
Jarres de Canaan,
Fouilles rituelles en bronze des temples,
Pilons, meules et mortiers –
Tout me ramène à toi
Devant ta vielle balance rouillée
Au Mouski au Caire, par la menthe parfumée.
Je me souviens de ton bureau beige-orange,
Avec Tohami le sourd
Pesant les sacs de farine lourds –
Et moi, écoutant le cri des oiseaux
Piaillant l'alarme dans la charpente:
«Sois vif, vite juif errant,
Ouvre tes yeux, juifs
Car il te faudra
Encore une fois
Bientôt t'envoler …»

A voir ce flot de grain doré
Dans le silo de Dagon couler,
Sous les bras puissants des grues géantes,
Mes yeux s'emplissent de graines,
Car tu n'es pas là avec moi
Pour contempler ce beau spectacle –
Terre que tant tu aimais,
Mais où tu n'es pas enterré.

Pour toi cher père,
Je plante aujourd'hui un champs de blè,
Pour toi,
Qui toujours nous enseignais
Comment semer.

UNE SEMAINE VERTE

Semaine de menthe fraiche
semaine verte
jusqu'aux racines de l'être
semant son arome parfumée –
Gomatek khadra, qu'elle soit toute verte,
ta semaine verte
annoncait triomphalement mon père
le samedi soir au Caire
En nous donnant
sa bonne bénédiction
de retour des *Portes du Paradis,*
la grande synagogue de la rue Adli.

Que ta semaine soit toute verte,
disait-il rayonnant en passant
la branche de menthe parfumée
au-dessus de nos têtes enthousiasmées
Et surtout – n'oubliez pas de la retourner
toute en fleur –
au monde entier!

Qui me donnera une semaine verte
maintenant qu'il n'est plus?
maintenant que les *Portes du Paradis*
sont fermees?

Seule la paix – seule la paix
De menthe fraiche.

Je consacre le suivant poème à la mémoire de ma chère mère tant aimée – Fortunée Hemsi Yadid (Diday), du Caire et de Paris

MAMICA

Tu conaissais l'*Emile* de Rousseau
D'instinct, par coeur,
Tu nous laissais trotter pieds nus,
Dans les chaumes dorés,
Dormir fenêtres grandes ouvertes
Tu nous donnais tout ce que tu avais
De tes deux mains pleines,
Parfois tu oubliais de manger –
Jamais de nous nourrir,

Tous nos actes et paroles
Avaient pour toi l'éclat du diamant,
Tes enfants étaient tes petits dieux.
Même quand je t'ai quittée
Et quitté la France,
Pour un pays que j'aimais,
Tu n'as montre ni peine ni colère,
Tu as donne ta fille au kibboutz
Avec un sourire, suivi de larmes.

Aujourdh'ui, en retour, nous te bénissons
Comme une reine,
Sortant du coeur du métro parisien,
Auréolée d'amour,
Mami, mamica, fille des vagues,
A la belle plage de Bat-Galim,
Comme auparavant à Alexandrie,
Souriante sur un coquillage,
Reine couronnée d'amour.

*Mamica : Petite maman en Ladino.

Ada and her mother, Fortunée, at the Sea in Bat Galim

Le poème suivant j'adresse à mon amie d'école, Kadreya Fayoumi.
Nous êtions ensemble en classe, à l'école anglaise Alvernia, dans le
quartier de Zamalek, au Caire. Je me souvient attendrissement de
l'édition, que nous assurions, du magazine littéraire de l'école, The
Rainbow – l'Arc En Ciel. Deja, à ce jeune âge, mon amie musul-
mane et moi, nous exprimions ensemble notre profond désir de
paix et l'abolition des guerres.

De Haifa au Caire proche lointain

Je me souviens du sirop sucre de canne velouté
qu'ensemble nous buvions
dans la douceur de l'air bleuté,
sous des cieux ouverts,
des graines de tournesol
qu'ensemble nous craquions,
avec des plaisanteries
rires faisant écho ensolleillé
dans le soleil.

Qu'elles étaient délicieuses
les patates douces grillées
en ces jours d'arc-en-ciel dorés
et des ravissantes poupées
de sucre toutes enveloutées!
Mais contrairement à toi, chere Kadreya,
amie de mes jours de classe ensoleillés,
on m'a dit que je n'étais
qu'un oiseau de passage,
rien qu'une visiteuse –
bien que née sur la terre du Nil.

Par l'Egypte incitée,
mes ailes juives j'ai déployé
en quête d'un nouveau nid.
Sur le Mont Carmel, je l'ai trouvé
et suis décidé d' y rester.

Aujourd'hui mon désir premier
est que nos fils soldats, soient baignés
des rayons de paix, par leurs mères créés,
quand plus jeunes qu'eux elles étaient
aux jours d'arc-en-ciel si proches –
si lointains.

Siniora My New Friend in Gaza (In Italian)

La mia nuova amica siniora a Gaza

Il tuo sorriso timido sotto il veldo
E i tuoi occhi chiaroshuri sulla
Scenda della vita, della contesa, hanno preso
Il mio squardo
Ne Centro del Talenti di
Khan Yunis, a Gaza.

Ti ho invitata a fare una foto
Con noi
E tu d`invanto hai ancettato. Ti
Ho dato il mio libro di poesie della pace
Tradotto in arabo
Hai letto e hai detto:
"Ami la pace quanto io l'amo!"

Mi hai dato il tuo indirizzo, per
Altri mei libri, poi hai fissato
Al di là della finestra i
Nuovi, sbalorditivi, ediffici i di
Gaza, ed assorta hai mormorato:

"Dobbiamo constrruine la Palestina
Ance con le poesie della pace" e siamo
Diventale amiche.
Tra donne è cosi.

Mi hai chiesto dei miei figli
Ed io della tua famiglia,
Dei tuoi progetti,
Mi hai mostrato i tuoi lavori,
Ed io i miei scritti, le mie foto,
Mi hai mostrato la tua impressionante
Collezione di abiti palestinesi
Dai ricami sfarzosi.

Dolcemente hai chiesto: "Quale
Ti piace di più?"
Ho mirato quello blu scuro
Dai ricami rossi,
Come quello che solevano indossare in
Egitto, molto tempo fa.

"La ricamerò per te, e
Te lo manderò ad Haifa" hai risposto
Subito ma con delicatezza.
Ero cosi commossa e ti ho
Abbracciata, mia cara Siniora,
Mia nuova amica di Gaza.

Quando il nostro autobus blu è ripartito,
Avamo entrambe la lacrime agli occhi,
Mia meravigliosea nuova amica di Gaza.
Tra donne è una cosa favile,
Naturale, umana, è cosi.

Uomini! Imparate a cambiare
Dalle Donne.
Lasciate che le donne vi aiutiono
A fare pace, a diventare amici.
Tra donne è una cosa facile,
Naturale, umana, è cosi.

(Traduzione di Allesandro Lovinelli)

Ada Aharoni

Quiero matar a tu guerra

I Want To Kill You War (in Spanish)

Quiero matar a la guerra, para siempre,
no como un ave fénix, que siempre vuelve!
Quiero matar a la guerra y no sé cómo!
Y yo no sé por qué todos los pueblos del mundo
no unen las manos para matar a la guerra ...,
Es el mayor asesino!

Los gobernadores de todo el mundo
viven aumentando su grasa abdominal
con los nuevos soldados y las armas nucleares.
Con los ojos borrosos sólo saben colgar
a uno o dos asesinos tal o cualpero la guerra
que ellos promueven
es el mayor asesino universal!

Después de la carnicería, el sacerdote dijo:
"Todos somos responsables".
Después de la matanza el jeque dijo:
"Todos somos como hermanos".
Después de la carnicería el rabino dijo:
"Podemos detenerlo si así lo decidimos."
El sacerdote y el jeque y el rabino
Levantan las manos y miran hacia el cielo!

Los manifestantes de la paz echan mano de la losa de mármol
En la que se lee "Queremos vivir, no morir"
y se la llevan bajo las balas zumbando ay que horror
como un cadáver, aún caliente, aún con vida –
Todavía deseo de crear un nuevo mundo bajo el sol
un mundo pleno de armonía y amor.

Traducido por Maria Cristina Azcona

Ada Aharoni

Fred er en kvinne og en mor

Peace Is Woman and A Mother (In Norwegian)

Hvordan kan du vite
At freden er en kvinne?
Jeg vet for visst,
Fordi jeg møtte henne i går
På min krokede vei
Til verdens markedsplass.
Hun hadde et slikt sørgmodig ansikt
Lik en gylden famlet blomst
Før den visner

Jeg spurte henne hvorfor
Hun var så trist?
Hun fortalte at hennes barn
Var drept i Auschwitz,
Hennes datter i Hiroshima,
Og hennes sønner i Vietnam,
Irland, Israel, Palestina, Libanon,
Pakistan og India,
Bosnia, Rwanda og Tsjetsjenia

Alle de andre av hennes barn, fortalte hun
Sto på den kjernefysiske drapsliste
Med mindre hele verden forstår –
At freden er en kvinne.
Tusen lys vil da skinne
I hennes funklende øyne, og da så jeg –
Freden er i høyeste grad en gravid kvinne,
Freden er en mor.

"Peace is a Woman", gjendiktet til norsk av Lars Chr. Sande.

Ada Aharoni

Tali My Rare flower (in Spanish)

Tali mi bella flor rara

Qué terrible falta de justicia! Qué dolor!
Te educamos para el amor, la honestidad y la generosidad,
Para honrar la vida, la paz y la humanidad –
Y así es como has crecido, así es como has vivido,
Un ángel en la tierra,
Una bella flor, rara, arrancada antes de tiempo!
Qué terrible falta de justicia! Qué dolor!

Eras sabia, con un corazón de oro, hermosa y con gran talento!
A pesar de tus sufrimientos dolorosos, debido a tu cáncer cruel,
Nunca te quejaste, nunca lloraste,
Seguiste cuidando a tu familia con cariño y devoción,
Para bailar y cantar, para dirigir tu excelente "Coro Nofit",
Y para dar una conferencia sobre la
"Importancia del Desarrollo de la Memoria"
En el ejemplar Instituto "Dorot" que se fundó en Galilea.

Tu esposo maravilloso y tres hijos
E incluso la pequeña y dulce Lotem tu primera nieta,
te ayudaron a soportar el dolor.
Todos nos quedamos para sentir tu mano suave, noble hasta el
amargo final. Qué terrible falta de justicia! Qué dolor!

Incluso entonces, nos diste valientemente tu sonrisa encanta-
dora, con la esperanza, y así es como siempre te recuerdo Tali, mi
flor hermosa y rara…
Descansa en Paz.

tu madre amorosa
Ada

Mi hija maravillosa, Tali Aharoni Winkler, quien disfrutó de una
vida totalmente dedicada y fructífera, murió de cáncer en los
huesos, el 8 de julio de 2011 tras una valiente lucha por dieciséis
años largos y llenos de acontecimientos.

Traducido por Maria Cristina Azcona

A Green Week (in Spanish)

Una Semana Verde

Una semana como menta fresca,
una semana verde que esparce su perfume
en las raíces de mi ser.

"Tengan una semana verde!"
Mi padre decía para bendecirnos el sábado noche

"Tengan un año verde" él
emitía, blandiendo un ramito nuevo fresco
sobre cabezas rizadas – y lo devolvía
al mundo completamente florecido.

Quién me dará una semana verde
ahora que él está muerto?
Ahora que las Puertas del Cielo se cierran,
y descargamos nuestros desechos nucleares grisáceos
en las profundidades de vientre
de nuestra tierra verde
inocente?

Sólo ciencia de paz
Sólo tecnología de paz
Sólo paz, hagamos un mundo
más allá de la Guerra.

Traducción Maria Cristina Azcona

PART TEN

PEACE LETTERS

LETTER TO KADREYA: FROM HAIFA TO CAIRO WITH LOVE

Dear Kadreya,

I have often thought of writing to you, there is so much we could tell each other after twenty years of life in "enemy countries." Tonight, when I finally take up my hesitating pen between my fingers–though the gap over distance, time, and perhaps values, still looms forbiddingly–with the Peace Treaty between our two countries, Egypt my former country, and Israel my present one, I discern a shaft of hope, a possibility of renewed ties between us. Over the oceans of prejudice and blunder, I feel tonight that I can at long last extend my hand to you in a craving for understanding and open friendship.

As I write, I see again my pensive school chum Kadreya of "Alvernia English School for Girls" in Zamalek, with her pale-olive tan, her serious deep gray eyes, and her charcoal curls of weblike softness glistening in the sun. What a bunch of active, tenacious and bright kids we must have been then to be able to write and publish a "literary" magazine all on our own at the age of thirteen! Do you remember the joys and heartaches "The Rainbow" gave us as co-editors? And the oath we solemnly took then to become writers when we grew up, so as "to do good to mankind, and banish wars from the earth forever"? How delightfully uncomplicated, naive, and enthusiastic we were then!

The last time I saw you was in 1949, when you came to bid me farewell before we left for France. My father, Jewish and a French national, had his business permit withdrawn. You whispered wistfully–I can almost hear your tremulous voice–"Why are you leaving Egypt? You were born here, this is your country!"

I couldn't explain then what I shall try to do tonight twenty-five years later, that for me, unlike you, Egypt was not my country. The first powerful impact of that stark fact hit me full in the face when I was only seven years old. This is a part of my childhood that I don't like to remember, as it has left a sore spot in my mind even after all this time, but I feel I have to try to communicate this experience to you as it might lead us towards a better understanding. That forlorn, dazed child, whom I shall try to conjure up, is so remote from me today that I can only recall her in the third person.

A frail girl of seven was being led wide-eyed and hesitant through the bustling narrow streets of Bab-El-Louk Souk, by a tall, hefty maid, Mohsena. The child was worried and confused; instead of taking her to the park for her usual afternoon stroll, the maid had furtively led her to this sordid and unknown world. The child drew back her small hand reluctantly but the maid pulled it firmly, announcing impatiently from time to time, "We shall soon be there."

"But where?" asked the child querulously for the tenth time. "Don't ask questions again, you will soon see," answered the maid abruptly and she energetically plodded on.

With growing fear, the little girl looked forlornly around her. She was sure the sun had been shining when she left home, but here in the tortuous smelly streets it was dark. On every side of the dirty streets vendors in colored striped cloaks shouted their modulated guttural utterances: "Er-essus, Er'r'essus, Tamar Hindi, Ter-mess, Ter-rrrmess"; and ragged beggars pushed against the terrified child.

Above the general din, one refrain became more and more distinct, and the bewildered little girl became aware she was being addressed: "Affrangeia, affrangeia what are you doing here?"

She felt the insult in the word affrangeia; but why were they insulting her? She had never seen these people before, and there they stood grimacing at her and hating her for no reason at all!

Even Mohsena seemed different; from her usually cheerful submissive self she had become incommunicative, bent on her private pursuits, unknown and unshared by the child. Her lips were firmly set, which made them look thin and pale, and her habitual easy bustle had changed into a nervous agitation.

The word affrangeia, however, was repeated so often and in such a variety of vindictive tones, that the child who scarcely dared address the maid in her new mood, finally asked, "Mohsena, what does affrangeia mean?"

The maid turned on her and curtly expostulated: "Didn't I tell you not to ask any more questions?"

The little girl felt more and more forlorn and gradually the sickening feeling inside her seemed to spill over and overwhelm her. She stopped, refused to go on, and pleaded tearfully: "I want to go back home now; I want my mamma."

"We shall soon be there," came the prompt and decisive retort, and she was pulled firmly along again, through what seemed to be an unending nightmare.

The child gazed mournfully at the hectic activity around her. Some ragged barefoot children had tied an old baby bathtub to a hanging pole and were swinging it dangerously, while a screaming boy inside it madly gesticulated to the mocking children to stop. As soon as they saw the little girl however, the bathtub was forgotten, and pointing menacing fingers at her, the noisy bunch circled around her shouting the same infuriating chant of affrangeia, affrangeia. She fled, and a tear flowed down her cheek.

The painful odyssey continued. The dazed child started to wonder if something strange had happened to her in the last half-hour, something she was not aware of but which had rendered her so despicable that everybody stared at her in amazement. She furtively touched her ears and backside. "Had she suddenly grown ears and a tail like Pinocchio?" But this clutching fear subsided as her trembling hands moved over her ears, and she breathed in relief. Suddenly she was arrested by a horrible cry, piercing her ears. She felt a chill creeping up her spine, a warning in her blood that violence and mutilation were in the air.

On the pavement before her a young shaggy donkey had laid his bleeding head while a bunch of rollicking, barefooted brats were lashing his back and behind. The donkey's large brown liquid eye stared at the child's pale face, and again it emitted a long heart-rendering heehaw. The child had never heard or seen anything like it before. The hideous scene seemed to be in some strange manner linked with her own misery and part of her own experience. She couldn't keep silent any longer. She tore her hand away from the maid, and shouted with all the power of her young lungs, "Stop, stop, you're killing him!"

The boys stopped in surprise, then, noticing the frail little girl they waved their whips threateningly: "Affrangeia, go away, what business is it of yours? Or do you want to taste our whips too?"

The sight of the donkey's blood pouring from his wounds over-whelmed the child and she burst out in trembling defiance, "I'm not affrangeia, I'm not, you're affrangeia all of you!" She was still screaming at the astonished children when Mohsena swiftly carried her away. The maid seemed somewhat more affable now; she wiped the child's tears and said in a soothing voice, "We're here now; that's it, it's this nice shop with the pretty sugar dolls, I told you we'd get here in no time, didn't I?"

The little girl's sobbing gradually subsided, and she gazed with wonder at the rows and rows of white and brown sugar dolls of all sizes dressed in gaily colored sparkling paper. With tear-stained face she stared at the expressionless multitude. Here at least was a silent world that did not threaten to "affrangeia her". The shop-owner, who seemed to be the maid's lover, beamed with flaming face at the now coy and strangely excited Mohsena, while he reiterated under his profuse mustache, "Welcome, *Ahlan Wesahlan*," with overdone cordiality. He patted the child mechanically on the head and said off- hand, "You brought the little affrangeia to visit us, heh?"

This time the evil word was so unexpected that the little girl just stood there petrified and looked at him unbelievingly.

"What's the matter?" laughed Mohsena nervously, annoyed at the stare. "Affrangeia is not an insult!"

The man guffawed, "Is this why she gapes at me so? I thought I had trod on her toes or something."

"What's affrangeia?"

"It means," the man explained gallantly, "European."

"What?" the child asked in unbelieving dismay, not comprehending how this could apply to her.

"It means that you are not an Arab like us," he continued con-descendingly. "Your face is white, not brown like ours; you are a foreigner, a stranger."

"But I was born in Cairo; my parents were born here – I'm not affrangeia, I'm not!"

"There's no reason for you to cry," said the man soothingly, throwing meaningful, amused looks at Mohsena, "If you want to think you're not then you're not, but how will you convince others?"

With that he stopped bothering with her, and turned his exclusive attention towards Mohsena.

So that was it, she was different, she was an outsider, a stranger, and she could do nothing about it. Whatever she would do she would never be able to convince anybody in the land where she was born that it was not so, she would always be considered a foreigner, an intruder, and a freak.

She sighed sadly at the new revelation, and yearning for the warmth of her protected life at home; she looked for consolation at the crowded rows of white and brown dolls. "You will not tell your parents that Mohsena brought you here, will you?" asked the man with a suave smile. "Here, I'll give you a nice *Muled El Nabi* doll and we'll forget we were here, won't we? They're for the feast of our prophet Mohamed, our *Nabi*. I'll raise you up so you can pick one yourself," he said coaxingly, "You'd like that, wouldn't you?"

The child saw all the dolls staring at her face indifferently, and she grabbed the nearest, a brown one with a green and white outfit.

"Are you sure you want a brown one?" the man asked slyly gazing at her intently, "I think it's preferable to have one of your kind," he said with a wink at Mohsena, and grabbing the dark doll he exchanged it for a white one wearing a white robe with sky blue stripes, and a shining Star of David over her forehead. The child pressed the sugar doll to her quivering lips, and its taste was sweet.

The whole traumatic experience related above had a very powerful effect on me and on my attitude to life, in spite of my tender age. After that painful revelation, my first "Epiphany", I spent most of my life in Egypt until we left, trying to figure out where I belonged.

If I was not an Egyptian, what was I? Though my mother tongue was French and we were of French nationality, I did not feel French; I had an English culture for I was in an English school since I was a tot, and I had fallen deeply in love with English literature, but again I did not feel English. Thus my roots not being tucked in any soil, dangled painfully in the air, unprotected, sending spasms of uncertainty and emptiness through my being.

By 1948, to the word affrangeia was added the more spiteful and emotionally laden one of *tsahiuneia* "Zionist", which was often hissed at me for no reason at all, for I was not a Zionist then. I got my bitter taste of anti-Semitism, and it brought back the revulsion I had felt when I first discovered that I was different and did not belong.

Now the yearning to identify, to become part of something bigger and more important than just myself, became still more acute. I yearned for the birthright of every human being: for a country where I could feel "this is my land, I belong to it, and it belongs to me; this is where I mean to plant my roots, and here nobody will tell me I do not belong!"

After we had to leave Egypt in 1949, in France, I found no solution to my identity problem. My general unrest was rather diffuse. As you can well understand, it was very hard for such a young girl to put her finger on the right spot among a multitude of others and say, here, this is precisely where it hurts.

When I talked to my family about my strange "malaise," this uncomfortable, gnawing feeling of being where I did not belong and with which I could not identify myself however hard I tried, they laughed and belittled my ears. "So what? You're not the only wandering and uprooted Jew. We're all like that and always will be." My spirit revolted against this placid injunction. "Why always?" I asked at first incredulously and then, as time went on, more and more obstinately. Seeking solutions to counteract the "always" I started to look towards Israel, the young Jewish state.

One day, I was trying to hitchhike to the Cote d'Azure together with a French friend. A driver slowed down and thrusting his head from his window shouted at us *"sales youpins!"*

Puzzled, I asked my friend what *"youpin"* meant.

"Oh, it's just a French derogatory word for Jews, like 'yid' or 'kike', you know," she explained lightly." I don't pay any attention to that kind of thing anymore, you have to learn to live with it, they're not all like that, thank God! France is a very liberal country, and the Jews in it can live their lives in peace if they don't take every silly expression to heart." That night I couldn't sleep, and the old fears wracked my brain and heart. I decided at length that I couldn't and wouldn't "live with it."

Seeking solutions to counteract the "always", I decided I wanted to become a pioneer in the new two year–old Israel and help it to grow. In 1950, I left my family in Paris and came to Israel, alone, at the age of sixteen. Here at last, to my boundless joy, I found that I belonged. I took to the country and it took to me; I planted my roots deeply in it and they bore fruit. This does not mean there were no problems of adaptation. I had to learn a new language and absorb a new culture, and I suffered all the characteristic difficulties of periods of transition. But I felt that I was wanted, that at long last I was home, and that wonderful new feeling of belonging magically smoothed the jagged path.

Today, I feel myself an Israeli in the full sense of the word. The problems of my country are my problems, and everything that happens here means and means intensely. Life becomes so much richer and more significant when you do not live it only for yourself and for your narrow family circle. So you see, dear Kadreya, Israel just had to exist, for rootless people with a hurting lack of clear identity, like me. For me, Israel was, and is to this day, a most profound existential need.

My son is due to go into the army next week, and if a Peace Treaty between our two countries is not signed soon, he may perhaps one day be facing yours, and they might both see death in each other's eyes! This is not the bright future we had planned for them in our brave little magazine "The Rainbow", years and years ago, when we were younger than they are today. The whole absurd situation we find ourselves in nowadays seems to me to be so senseless and unnecessary!

Having told you all this, I suddenly feel very near to you dear Kadreya. I would very much like to see you and chat with you at length again as we often did in the past. Perhaps somehow, some day, this wish may become a reality, and we shall be able to meet again in peace and friendship on the calm banks of the magnificent

Nile, or among the green splendors of my beloved Mount Carmel in Haifa.

With deepest wishes for peace,

Yours sincerely,
Ada Aharoni

(Former Andree, Ada Yadid)

*This is an autobiographical Letter,
as well as the following poem.*

Ada Aharoni

From Haifa to Near Faraway Cairo

I recall the velvet sugar-cane juice
we drank together
with the smooth blue air
under the open skies,
the sunflower seeds
we cracked together
with jokes
echoing laughter in the sun.
How sweet the roasted sweet-potatoes
were in those rainbow days
of pretty sugar dolls.

But unlike you, dear Kadreya,
Friend of my sunny schooldays,
I was told that I was just
a visiting guest
though born in the land of the Nile.
Ordered by Egypt my Jewish wings
to spread
to search for a new nest,
I have found it on Mount Carmel
and here I mean to stay.

My foremost wish today
is our soldier sons
to bathe
in the peaceful rays
their mothers wove
when younger than they
in the near faraway
Rainbow Days.

Ada Aharoni's class at Alvernia-Zamalek school, in the first and
second row, and a senior class in the upper rows.
(Ada is the fifth from left, first row)

Letter to President Anwar Sadat
and Mrs. Jehan Sadat

Cairo, Egypt   25 October 1977

Dear President Anwar Sadat and Mrs. Jehan Sadat,

I am enclosing a poem and an autobiographical letter entitled: "Letter to Kadreya: from Haifa to Cairo with Love," both addressed in particular to a dear school-friend of mine in Cairo, whose name in 1949 was Kadreya Fayoumi, and in general to the women of Egypt.

May the Interim Sinai Accord lately signed between our two countries, Egypt and Israel, be the opening of a massive gate to a Peace Treaty between Egypt and Israel, and a massive gate to a real peace in the whole of the Middle East.

These poem and letter are modest attempts to extend a hand in Salam-Shalom to you both, Mr President and Mrs. President, to Kadreya and to the women and men of Egypt, whom I remember with warmth.

As we were friends in the past, there is no valid reason we cannot be friends in the future too, when as we all hope, our two countries will, with mutual trust and good–will, reach a real and lasting peace.

With deepest wishes for true Salaam–Shalom,

Yours sincerely,
Dr. Ada Aharoni
Haifa, Israel

Forty five years after she left school and Egypt, Ada Aharoni received the following two beautiful letters from her former teacher of literature and headmistress of her school, Sister Mary Odile.

First of Two Letters from Sister Mary Odile,
Headmistress of Alvernia English School, in Zamalek, Cairo

To Ada Andree Aharoni

30 October, 1996

Dear Andree Ada Aharoni,

Julie Andrews it was in her famous Musical, "The Sound of Music," declared that "The Beginning is a very good place to start." The veracity of this statement is happily borne out in her melodious rendering of the first three letters of the Alphabet: A, B, C. My introductory choice, however, issues from different soil, sacred soil, the soil of Israel itself. It is the Psalmist who speaks, speaks to you Andree, speaks to me, speaks as Yahweh would have him speak following the pattern of the last verse of Psalm 33.

What more compelling proof of Yahweh's love for each of us, than the fact that after a span of forty five years (yes forty five years), I am still here, joyously engaged in penning a nineteenth century type of letter to the now literary renowned Dr. Ada Aharoni, my cherished student of the unforgettable unforgotten Rainbow Days!

Now Andree, fond memories surface. Somewhere in Anthony and Cleopatra, Anthony refers to his *"salad days, when I was green in judgment ..."* Having found you a literary peer in Shakespeare, let me now tell you that my true reaction to the sheer beauty of your verse brought me back to the sheer delights of a Shelley and Keats,

> *A thing of Beauty is a joy forever: its loveliness increases; it will*
> *never pass into nothingness ...*   John Keats

Neither will yours Andree. Undoubtedly, Shelley's Skylark is a creature of cosmic dimension but lacks the human touch, the maternal grace so aptly expressed by your Mother Bird. Nor is there any *"maiden with green eyes and dark lashes"* introduced to be the harbinger *"for songs and for laughter."* On the contrary, Shelley's maiden is

> *High-born*
> *In a palace tower*
> *Soothing her love-laden*
> *Soul in secret hour ...*

And in your moving poem *Israel:*

> *To leave you now*
> *would be an*
> *amputation –*
> *I would survive*
> *but there would*
> *be*
> *less*
> *of me*

Why? Because as is said in *"Songs of Songs"*: "Deep waters cannot quench love nor floods sweep it away." May I also add that this your briefest poem, blissfully binds into one: healer, healing, healed.

A poem of yours with which I feel the truest empathy–a truly nostalgic call, is that which does reverence in poetically traveling *From Haifa to Near Faraway Cairo.* As we say in Ireland: "It raises the cockles of my heart!" How I enjoy the mere joy of just writing and experiencing within myself the following:

The sunflower seeds
we cracked together
with jokes
echoing laughter in the sun.
How sweet the roasted sweet potatoes
were in those rainbow days
of pretty sugar dolls …

THEN BANG!

Ordered by Egypt
my Jewish wings to spread
to search for a new nest –
I have found it on Mount Carmel
and here I mean to stay.

Good for you Andree!

Incarnate, in verse three, of this beautiful poem, it seems to me, is the replica of "the constant love and deep devotion" bestowed on you by your mother, Fortunee Diday, that now becomes the enriching heritage of your soldier son. Even there linger those unforgotten, unforgettable "*near faraway rainbow days.*"

Other lines that touch me deeply within, are embodied in your noble empathy with the "Egyptian Soldier."

You see Egyptian Soldier,
You will always have your Nile and your Baled
To turn to,

297

> *But if we lose*
> *There is only the sea....*

Thank you Dr. Ada Aharoni, for having treated us to the vision rather than the actuality of seeing *"Horses on Ennismore Gardens."* With true Shakespearian éclat you have (to my mind), carried your theme beautifully from beginning to an unexpected rhetorical end: "But I never saw the horses on Ennismore Gardens." Bard, not of Avon, but of the Thames, would I proudly nominate you, Andree, ingenious student of mine!

Now back to your Magnificent Nile and the terra firma of "Alvernia English School, in Zamalek." You have expressed the truth yourself in your "Letter to Kadreya," that you were "a bunch of active, tenacious and bright kids". Yes, but so infinitely more were you! Forty five years later, I thank and commend yourself and Kadreya for your joint literary achievement as thirteen-year-olds. Even in the world of letters the saying: "coming events cast their shadows before," contains more than a grain of truth. Right there on the hard ground of Alvernia English School, you grasped, held, questioned those aspects of life accessible to you. Wisely, you and Kadreya separated "the wheat from the chaff," thus laying the foundation of the development of the multi-faceted, humanistic warm–hearted peace–loving poet and ingenious author that you have become. Let us cling to the hope that indeed one day soon, as you yearn for in your poem: *"Mimosa Flowers"* "the sun will shine on all mortals with equal golden rays."

To this I add a prayer–that the yet unborn citizens of the 21st century will be more accepting and kinder towards one another, than have been our confrères of the dwindling 20th. Within the realm of hope lies the possibility of East and West actualizing the significance of the *"Olive Branch"*. Thereby Ghandi Mohandas Karamachand, Dr. Martin Luther King, and Dr. Ada Aharoni, would receive the honor of befitting them as Messengers of Peace unto their own people, place and time.

For unavoidable reasons, I had to lay this humble commentary on your impeccable masterpiece aside, for a while, so to quick up the dominant thread again is not easy. Your autobiographical "Letter to Kadreya", to use an American phrase, "is out of this world!" It is really worthy of great admiration, the well–balanced splendor of your English prose, the ingenuity of your arresting figures of speech, endowed as they are with the capacity to arouse empathy of any kind.

Oh! Andree, you poor little hurting child, how can you stand there as a bruised reed of Mother Nile and endure all of this insolence? Truth is, you didn't stand for long–you ran and ran. Out of sympathy for a creature in distress–the donkey, you identified with his pain. How true the old saying: "A fellow feeling makes us wondrous kind." In the arms of your loving Mama you desired consolation, peace, reassurance..."

With the aptitude of a psychologist, you have given us a true-to-life and down-to-earth account of the effects of the Bab-El-Louk trauma on your later growth and development. Thankful am I Andree, that your days at Alvernia were "sunny" and above all else that "you fell so deeply in love with English Literature." That first true love of yours was not just an emotional alleviation then, but (in my unlicensed language), has since led you to the stars!

Other poems too I would like to delve into – Manna for a later day! While in the shower the other night, I heard myself humorously reciting:

Abdul's Children will not know more than Abdul does
for Abdul's children are not taught more than Abdul was ...

I treasure your book as I do the Bible. Each in its way shares the relationship between God, Humanity, and Mother Earth... Of my future reactions to other of your poems, I shall keep you posted. The members of the Provincial Administration felt so proud that Alvernia School had produced a student of your caliber. They would appreciate a copy of "Poems from Israel," to be kept with worthwhile treasures in the Community Archives in Boston.

I too happen to have a treasure: a copy photograph of your sister Ginette, as cherub - when second grader, and the Ginette, 45 years later,who appeared in London in 1996, at their class reunion (thanks to Viviane Biriotti and Denise).

Very pleased am I, Andree, to know that among the green splendors of your beloved Mount Carmel, you have found peace, may it always remain this way. In the early 1940's, when Egypt was in danger of the German invasion, we, then sisters from St. Clare's, in Heliopolis, were evacuated to what was then called Palestine. We spent three months in a beautiful green area above Jerusalem, the name sounded something like *"Qubebeh,"* which, if I remember properly, was somehow associated with "bread." The evacuation occurred in June, however, after having had a vacation, including pilgrimages to the sacred places, we were safely back in Heliopolis, in time for another school year in September.

Thank you Andree, for who you are, for what you have become, and for remembering me.

Sister Mary Odile who loves you

SECOND LETTER OF SISTER MARY ODILE

December 24, 1996

Dear Andree Ada,

For the literary wealth of the precious packet you mailed to me a few weeks ago "Thanks." From within the soul of the soul of the six letters conveniently comprising that conventional word (thanks), I wish to impart even in some infinitesimal way, the light, the life, the joy that your true Literature imparted to me.

I am sending you the picture of Wilfred Owen, the poet you so admire and who has so influenced you in your peace poems. His great poems of protest against the demonic War, and his powerful rhythms, touched deeply the hurting and conscientious spot in you Andree, while still at Avernia English School, almost half a century ago.

An as yet inexperienced emotion entered your being radiating light, joy and the worthiness of being alive. Something akin, maybe, to your own *"Horses on Ennismore Gardens."* I mean the moving sensation evoked by each of your poems. Mentally, you have been raised above the sordidness of the Souk, no reason to wallow there ever again… The healing process has long since begun, but as you have since experienced, Ada – it takes time!

For reasons I am about to tell you, I have not dealt with all the highly appreciated material you so generously sent me. I was glad to be able to share "Birth Pangs of Peace: In Memory of Yitzhak Rabin," with different kinds of people, and they all loved it. You are a true, powerful and dedicated Peace Poet.

To me it seems that one of the influences on your life has been the River Nile. Literally, you grew up on its banks. While contributing to the formation of the Delta, with its lore-laden waters, the Nile must have, in some mystic way, brought enrichment to your spirit too. To the Creator, Giver of all gifts, I give thanks for your innate giftedness. May the hopes and prayers of those who truly "care" be realized in the bestowal of the Nobel Prize in Literature on you, Ada, true proponent of "Peace through Literature"– you truly deserve it.

Now for the not so good news. I am scheduled for Heart-Surgery at the Medical Center Hackensack on January 7.

This will slow down things for a while, but with God's help, all will go well.

My Love to you and yours,

Sister Mary Odile

P.S. Often I have told students to avoid "P.S's" and then fall into the trap myself!

You write at the end of your *"Letter to Kadreya"*: "My son is due to go into the army next week, and if a Peace Treaty between our two countries is not signed soon, he may perhaps one day be facing yours, and they might both see death in each other's eyes! This is not the bright future we had planned for them in the Rainbow, years and years ago, when we were younger than they are today."

Congratulations that the girlish dreams of "the Rainbow days," have been fulfilled in your son, Ariel, who was destined to look for LIFE not death, in the eyes of other human beings, and that is probably why he has chosen to become a gynecologist who helps to deliver life. Creditably, your Daughter, Talia, too is involved in cultural life-giving activities. What a boon for "Grandma" to have the pleasure of feeling herself, lovingly caressed by six different pairs of hands in one day! Probably the innocence of these little children is a richer contribution to your professional life than you could even dream of. The real task of the poet, I read lately, is to get you somewhere you haven't been before…" You have done it Ada!

Thanks, and much Love,

Sister Mary Odile

In Memoriam Sister Mary Odile

Unfortunately, all did not go well during the heart surgery, and brave Sister Mary Odile passed away on January 7, 1997, in New Jersey, USA, from which she had sent her two letters.

In a great measure, I owe to her and to Sister Mary Consuela, of Alvernia School, and all the brave Franciscan Nuns who corrected our compositions every night with so much dedication and devotion, my love for humanity, for writing, for literature, and for peace.

The publishing of these two letters above, is in a small way my warm tribute and thanks to the memory of Sister Mary Odile, and to all my beloved teachers for having instilled in me deep values, and the love and recognition of the power of literature as a valuable vehicle that can help to create a better world beyond war. May Sister Mary Odile's memory be blessed, and may she rest in peace.

With much sorrow for the passing away of such a noble soul,

Sister Mary Odile's loving and faithful pupil,

Ada Andrée Aharoni

EPILOGUE:
BRINGING HEARTS TOGETHER

Ada Aharoni presenting her book *Bringing Hearts Together*, at the *Ahmedim* Mosque in Kababir in Haifa.

An Unforgettable Moment in a Mosque

The day I was invited
to greet the Ahmedim community
in their Kababir Mosque in Haifa –
I was sure it was a joke!
Me a woman, to address the audience
in their beautiful Islamic Mosque! Impossible!
Me a woman, and a Jewish woman at that!
I was doubly sure it was a joke.

But they called and reminded me gently
I was invited to address the audience
at their yearly Conference
on " Bringing Hearts Together",
in their Kababir Mosque.
On my tingling way to Kababir
I told my friends I was sure they would
invite me to speak in the back of their backyard -
no way it could be inside the Mosque!

The Ahmedim Imams talked about
"Love to All – and Hatred to None,"
and then, I was called to the Podium in the Mosque
and not outside in the yard!
I felt a stream of gladness sprouting in my veins
I couldn't believe it, and yet there I was
a messenger of peace in a community of peace.
My heart opened like a secret door on its hinges,
and I told them they are the hope of our region.

In the pictures of this unforgettable event,
I see the Imams at their table
behind me smiling hopefully,
while I quoted from my book bearing the
same title as their Conference – Kiruv Levavot.
I felt a fathomless joy,
I was in an Islamic haven of peace!

When the Ahmedim woman I didn't know
came and hugged me and said –
"You made history today!"
I felt I had opened the door for her too.

(Kababir, June 30, 2012)

*Composer and Singer Shoshia Beeri - Dotan with Ada
and Fatheya, at the Kababir Conference on :
"Bringing Hearts Together".*

ADA AHARONI RECEIVES THE PRESTIGIOUS PRESIDENT SHIMON
PERES AWARD FOR PEACE CULTURE AND FOR BRINGING JEWISH
AND ARAB HEARTS TOGETHER (4TH SEPTEMBER, 2012).
On the right, Prof. Menahem Ben-Sasson, President of the
Hebrew University in Jerusalem, head Judge and director of the
President Award Committee.

Itai, Tali's son, holding the President Shimon Peres Award, with Ada, Avi and Nitzan.

Ada with IFLAC Friends at the Shimon Peres Award Ceremony in the President's Garden in Jerusalem.

Other Books by Ada Aharoni

Aharoni A. (1979). From the Pyramids to Mount Carmel, Eked, Tel Aviv.

Aharoni A. (1983). The Second Exodus, Bryn Mawr: Pennsylvania. ISBN 0-8059-2862-6

Aharoni A. (1984). To Alexandria Jerusalem and Freedom, Pennsylvania, ISBN 0-8059-2922-3. (Published also in a Hebrew edition 1985, and an Arabic edition 1986, Mahmoud Abassi, Shfaram, Galilee, Israel).

Aharoni A. (1985). Shin Shalom: New Poems (A bi–lingual edition – Hebrew and English), Eked, Tel Aviv.

Aharoni A. (1985 to 2003) - Ten Volumes of GALIM Peace Culture and Literature Magazine, IFLAC, Micha Lachman, Haifa. ISBN 965-7204-04-6

Aharoni A. (1987). Metal et Violettes. Caracteres, Paris, France (Poems in French).

Aharoni A. ed. (1992) and Cronin G., Goldman, L., Saul Bellow: A Mosaic. New York: Peter Lang. ISBN 0-8204-1572-3

Aharoni A. ed. (1993). A Song to Life and to World Peace., ed. A. Aharoni et al. Jerusalem: Posner and Sons., Jerusalem (Jerusalem Books: jerboooks@netmedia.co.il). ISBN 965-219-013-6

Aharoni A. (1995). Peace Flower: A Space Adventure, 119 pp. Haifa: M. Lachman (Iflac: POB 9934, Haifa 34341, Israel). ISBN 965-9013930

Aharoni A. ed. (1997). Galim 8: Waves of Peace, In Memory of Yitzhak Rabin., IFLAC, Shfaram Galilee: Hatichon (Jerusalem Books: Tel. 972-2-6426576), ISBN 965-222-774-9. (In Hebrew, English and Arabic).

Aharoni A. (1999). From the Nile to the Jordan, 146 pp. (Available through Ada Aharoni - POB 16077, Nesher, Israel). ISBN 965-901-398-1

Aharoni, A. ed. (1996-1999). Horizon: Pave Peace, Peace Culture Online Magazine, nos. 1–5, IFLAC: The International Forum for the Literature and Culture of Peace. www.iflac.wordpress.com

Aharoni A. (2000). Peacemaking Through Culture: A New Approach to the Arab/Palestinian–Israeli Conflict, in Peace Studies from a Global Perspective: Human Needs in a Cooperative World, ed. Ursula Oswald Spring, pp. 252-280. Delhi: Maadhyam Book Services. maadhyam@india.com

Aharoni A. ed. (1999-2000). Women, Children and Peace. Horizon: Pave Peace, no. 4; The Online International Peace Research Association Anthology. www.iflac.wordpress.com

Aharoni. A (2002). Nashim Yotsrot Olam Mi ever la Milhamot ve la Alimout, Haifa: Micha Lachmann, ISBN 965-7204-01-1 (In Hebrew). Women Create A World Beyond War and Violence (Also available in Englsih - see below).

Aharoni, A. ed. (2003). Galim 10: New Waves 2000 Peace Culture Anthology, IFLAC: International Forum for the Literature and Culture of Peace, Haifa: M. Lachman, Jerusalem Books: jerbooks@netmedia.co.il. ISBN 965-902-900-4

Aharoni, A. (2004). You and I Can Change the World:, Peace Poetry, 99 pp. Haifa: Micha Lachmann. (Ada Aharoni - POB 16077, Nesher, Israel). ISBN 965-901-399X

Aharoni A. (2005). Women: Creating A World Beyond War and Violence, 120 pp. (Jerusalem Books: POB 26190, Jerusalem, Israel, 91261). ISBN 965-7204-00-3

Aharoni A. (2006). Du Nil Au Jourdain, Stavit: Litteratures d'Israel, Paris, France (Historical novel in French). ISBN 2-911671-75-9

Aharoni A. (2007) The Pomegranate: Love and Peace Poems, 1st Library Books, Indiana, USA.

Aharoni A. (2007). Nobel Laureate Saul Bellow's Inner Voice (Hebrew) - Pardess Publishing House, ISBN 965-7171-37-7

Aharoni A. (2008). Woman In White – Ha Isha BeLavan – (Hebrew) Micha Lachman. ISBN 965-90139-2-2

Aharoni. A. (2011). Bringing Hearts Together: A Novel About the Jews from Egypt (Hebrew) - Kiruv Levavot - Roman al yehudei Mitsrayim - Gvanim, Tel Aviv. ISBN 978-965-534-129-4

Aharoni A. (2012). Rare Flower: In Memory of my daughter Talia. (In Hebrew, Rimonim Publications, Israel). ISBN 0-6820000165-4

Most books are available on www.amazon.com

Biographical Sketch

Dr. Ada Aharoni is a writer, poet, and peace culture researcher. She writes in English, Hebrew, and French, and has published twenty–seven books to date some of which have been translated into several languages. She believes that culture and literature can help in healing the urgent ailments of our global village, such as war, terror, and famine. The themes of peace and conflict resolution toward the sustainability of our fragile earth, are major ones throughout her poetry and her works.

She studied at London University (England), where she received an M.Phil. in English Literature, on the novels of Henry Fielding, and at the Hebrew University (Jerusalem), where she received her Ph.D. degree on the works of Nobel laureate Saul Bellow. She taught Literature and Sociology at Haifa University, and in the Department of Humanities of The Technion: Israel Institute of Technology, as well as at the University of Pennsylvania.

Dr. Ada Aharoni is the Founding President of IFLAC*: The International Forum for the Literature and Culture of Peace, (1999). She has been awarded several international prizes and awards, and has been elected as one of the 100 Global Writer Heroines (Rochester N.Y. 1998). In September 2012 she received the President Shimon Peres Award, for the spreading of Peace Culture in the Middle East and in our global village.

---

* Readers who would like to join IFLAC for the promotion of a better world through Culture and Literature, can do so by visiting the following sites: www.iflac.com/ada, www.iflac.wordpress.com

ALPHABETICAL LIST OF POEMS AND LETTERS